HAPPY NESS

HAPPY NESS

LIFE LESSONS from a CREATIVE ADDICT

DR YUSUF MERCHANT

First published by Westland Publications Private Limited in 2018

61, 2nd Floor, Silverline Building, Alapakkam Main Road, Maduravoyal, Chennai 600095

Westland and the Westland logo are trademarks of Westland Publications Private Limited, or its affiliates.

Copyright © Dr Yusuf Merchant, 2018

ISBN: 9789386850980

10 9 8 7 6 5 4 3 2 1

The views and opinions expressed in this work are the author's own and the facts are as reported by him, and the publisher is in no way liable for the same.

All rights reserved

Typeset in Adobe Garamond Pro by SÜRYA, New Delhi
Printed at Thomson Press (I) Ltd.

No part of this book may be reproduced, or stored in a retrieval system, or transmitted in any form or by any means, electronic, mechanical, photocopying, recording, or otherwise, without express written permission of the publisher.

*for
the unsung hero
within you*

CONTENTS

Foreword ix
A Note on the Illustrations xiii

I. GIVE PEACE A CHANCE: THE BASICS — 1

1. Everything Is Perfect — 3
2. No Conditions Apply — 8
3. The Meaning of Life — 15
4. The Magic of Imagination — 29

II. MIND GAMES: THE FUNDAMENTALS — 37

5. The Ambulance Funda — 39
6. The Train Station — 44
7. The Paradoxical Pre-Intention Funda — 50
8. Even the Moon Has a Dark Side — 55
9. The Life Force, Within — 60
10. Shrink the Rascal — 65
11. The Spirit of Creation — 72
12. Frequencies Are Returned to Their Point of Origin — 80
13. Learnings from an Orange Tree — 86
14. Jaikishan & the Ant — 90

III. INSTANT KARMA: GETTING THERE — 103

15. Cervantes & the Ugly Duckling — 105
16. My Mother's Secret Marriage — 110
17. The Flavour of Love — 117
18. Thy Will Be Done — 121
19. An Event That Did Not Happen Changed My Life — 127
20. I Am Going to Die! — 134

21.	The Secret to Self-Confidence	142
22.	Two Sides to Reality	148
23.	Transformers	153
24.	The Eventual Reality	160
25.	The Commitment Funda	166
26.	Les Grands Manuels	173

IV. STARTING OVER: TRAINING THE MIND — 181

27.	Drugs, Alcohol and All That Buzz	183
28.	Destiny vs Free Will	188
29.	The Attention Fundamental	195
30.	A Conditioned Tool for Control	202
31.	The Fifth Dimension	206
32.	The Symbolism Funda	213
33.	Anger & Playing Dead	219
34.	No One Is Stupid	225
35.	The Traumatic Triangle	229
36.	Don't Celebrate Thought	235
37.	The Imagine-It Programme: The Power of 2 Per Cent	242

V. IMAGINE: IT'S EASY IF YOU TRY — 245

38.	My Patient Gurus	247
39.	The Solitary Universal Constant	251
40.	The Superior Race?	255
41.	The Word Little Is Not So Little	261
42.	The Power of I	267

Acknowledgements — 273

FOREWORD

IF YOU CAME HERE LOOKING FOR ONE OF THOSE SYRUPY volumes that help you deal with the grief of losing a pet turtle, this ain't it. Dead Turtle Therapy is over in Aisle 4.

Stories of people's lives are as countless as the stars, and as indiscriminate unless you get up close. Everybody has at least one—you have one, I have one, assorted uncles and aunts have a dozen apiece. The first time I met Yusuf 'Doc' Merchant, this is what I asked him: *Why should I listen to you?*

It was 2010 and I was a recent addition to the thirty-or-so residents of Land, a rehab facility neighbouring Mumbai city. 'Facility' is a terrible word to use here because it makes Land sound like something from a Michael Crichton thriller, all lab coats and security systems and dissected rodents. In truth, visually, Land is equal parts luxury mountain retreat and kitschy artist commune. There is a massive dining hall built almost entirely of shiny granite and marble. A gym. A swimming pool. Air-conditioned villas. There is also, squirrelled away like hazelnuts inside creamy chocolate, a wooden pagoda-style gazebo for prayer. A giant concrete PEACE symbol painted in electric pink. A junk chassis of an ancient jeep half buried in the ground.

The resulting mélange is a lot to take in.

Doc, perhaps unsurprisingly, given that he is the soul of the place, can be a lot to take in as well. He turned sixty last year but dresses like a teenager (expensive jeans with unorthodox stitching, trainers in neon candy colours). He eats, walks, speaks and laughs with an energy that pops and fizzes like a soda can gone mad. A believer of many and varied faiths, Doc is also irreverent in the extreme. I've seen him get cheeky with captains of industry, religious leaders, heads of institutions and the press corps alike, as if to say sure, we are speaking of important things but let's not take ourselves too seriously for fuck's sake! He never does, nor lets anyone else. His elfin sense of mischief seeks out and squashes any self-importance in the vicinity.

There are contradictions that become apparent: practically tone deaf himself, Doc is moved by music in any form and understands its emotional affect. Unequivocally masculine in his behaviour otherwise, he often breaks into tears mid-sentence because something has tapped into his deep vein of sentimentality (without wanting to promote a gender stereotype, it is undeniably rare to see a man do that— usually somebody has to die first). Though mellowed now by the passage of time, in the early days his mercurial temper would flash as suddenly as a summer storm. His wisdom is couched in stories that make you laugh, full of mimicry and physical comedy and multilingual cussing. Doc is, by any standard, a warm and genuine human being, and a performance artiste beyond compare.

So, June 2010. I was trying to quit a heroin habit that just wouldn't quit. You'd imagine that, defeated and messed up as I was, I would accept any offer of help without question. Uh-unh, not me. A minute after Doc had given me the nicest hug I could ever remember getting, I had a question: *Why should I listen to you, man?*

Affectionate as I am towards Doc now, in those days I was as hostile as dammit. I don't know what I expected in response. Perhaps he would tell me that he was a qualified doctor with over thirty years of experience in treating mental illness and substance abuse. Show me the news articles and UN reports that laud him as the spearhead of change in the field. Line up the several hundred families all over the world who would give personal testimony that he had saved the life of a loved one.

He didn't do any of that.

What he said was: *Don't. I give a fuck whether you listen to me or not.*

It sounds harsh, I know, but in that moment it was exactly what I needed to hear. It took the fight right out of me and I began to listen. Really listen. All change, all healing, begins with openness.

This is the—no other word for it—genius in a man. In knowing what to say to whom. Or, more accurately, in knowing that different people will be affected in different ways by the same story. Back in the 1980s, I had a poster of Michael Jackson's album *Bad* up on my wall. It showed a young Jackson dressed in that campy leather jacket, looking out at the world through his soft doe-eyes. Wherever I was in the room, those eyes followed me. It happens with certain posters or artwork sometimes, but I didn't know that then. I thought I was special—until my sister complained that the eyes tracked her too. And that's when I knew that it wasn't a quality in me that fascinated Michael Jackson so, but a quality in his poster that made me believe his eyes were for me alone.

Doc's stories, I've come to learn over the years, are like that. In person or in print, they mean different things to different people and, with each re-telling, they often mean different things to the same person. Whether you've picked up this book to learn a little self-awareness, or to find answers to specific questions, or simply to be entertained, chances are you will not be disappointed. Because when a person has lived as rich and chaotic a life as Doc has, their stories are gold.

ARJUN NATH

Author of *White Magic: A Story of Heartbreak, Hard Drugs and Hope*

A NOTE ON THE ILLUSTRATIONS

THIS BOOK HAS BEEN A LIFETIME'S JOURNEY FOR ME. DOC invited me to work on it with him at a fortuitous point in my life, when I most needed its insights and perspective.

At the time it seemed simple enough, but just another straightforward illustration assignment this wasn't. Much like the stories within this book—it's easy to intellectually understand them, but real transformation lies in practice. I, of course, thought I had it all figured out and over early readings and discussions with Doc, spoke abundantly in generalisations and platitudes. He persisted in nudging my focus inwards. *When have you felt this? How would you apply it to your life? What could your story become if you could see it afresh?*

Living at Land, that beautiful haven ensconced in the Malanggad mountains off Mumbai, I reflected on these questions and began drawing without prejudice or preconception. It was like dropping baggage and old beliefs at the door and letting an inner voice speak honestly, openly. Slowly transforming not only as an artist, but as a human being. I didn't create work to appeal or preach, I drew from life.

But while these drawings are mine, they are now also yours. See them as you will—as illustrations of ideas, whimsical visual musings or kick-starters to your own questions. Maybe if you will be so curious or generous, step into my universe awhile and play with the metaphors within. Return after you've finished reading the book and use them as a visual shortcut, a reminder.

And if you happen to find your own authentic voice polished along the way, in whatever form it may take for you, let's swap stories someday. That connection, to me, is real *Happyness*.

KRITI MONGA
Graphic designer and artist

I. GIVE PEACE A CHANCE

the basics

i want to remember to appreciate people and circumstances like i would a sunset or birdsong. without prejudice, control or need to understand. everything has its place, everything is meaningful, everything just is *

· CHAPTER I ·

'EVERYTHING is PERFECT'

'THE THIRD TREE IS OUT OF SYNC. THE OTHER SEVEN TREES are precisely aligned. If the third one wasn't drooping to the left side, they would make a flawless column,' I thought. The bark of the third tree was inclined roughly at an angle of 30 degrees with respect to the others. If that tree, too, had been aligned it would make a perfect row. They would be in an impeccable straight line.

When I looked more closely at the deviant tree, I saw that one of its lower branches was heavy, weighed down compared to the others. A strange thing happened then: once I'd understood the reason for the deviation, I stopped seeing it as a problem. I let my mind roam free, without questions or expectations, and was surprised to feel a sense of kinship with the 'out of sync' tree. The imperfection—that heavy branch, the sideways-leaning trunk—was actually beautiful in its own way. It was like me. Different.

Then I asked myself a question: 'Which tree is at an angle of 30 degrees?' Only the 'out of sync' tree; and if you were looking for an angled tree, it was no longer 'out of sync' or flawed, but perfect. The perfect answer would vary according to the question. Which of the trees is the shortest? The tallest? The most dense?

According to varying frames of reference, at any given point in time, most trees would be imperfect. But, when I thought about it some more, a surprising truth dawned upon me. They were all perfect. How was that possible?

Yes, all of the trees were perfect. Perfect in accordance with the laws of the universe. In the frame of reference of cause and effect. In the universal frame of reference, everything is flawless the way it is. Simply because it can't be anything else at that given point in time.

It's when we become the centre of the universe and our perceptions become the only frame of reference that we see things as imperfect. They probably are imperfect from our point of view. However, with a small or big shift in perspective, you'll see that most events, and people, are absolutely perfect.

When we are stationary on a highway, cars seem to pass by at high speeds. But when we are travelling in a car, in the same direction as the other cars, we see the vehicles beside us passing by at relatively slower speeds. The speed of the cars, in our frame of reference, is governed by the laws of physics. From our perspective they differ in speed. The contrasting speeds are relative to our frames of reference. Each perfect for its referential frame.

Once, on a trip to the mountains, I got nearly drowned—and I remember how time slowed down dramatically. That is because when our brain senses extreme danger, it grossly increases its inputs and processes the data at faster speeds. This results in time dilation. One experiences the event in slow motion—as I did.

But when I am with my daughter Bliss or my wife Sangita, time flies. Hours feel like minutes. So how should I perceive time? What is the correct sense of 'perfect' time? The time that I normally sense, the time that I experienced underwater, or the time I feel in the presence of my near and dear ones? They are all very distinct. They are all perfect time. Each circumstance calls for a different version of perfect.

It's perfect that all living beings die. Death is merely a

transition from one form to another. Everything is in a state of constant transformation; life forms are no exceptions. Can you imagine the madness if everything that had ever been born had never died? All plants and animals included. It would be terrifying, with everyone competing for scarce resources. If dinosaurs still roamed the earth, would we live the way we do (even if we existed)?

Our folly of attaching things to ourselves means that we often see events only from our own perspective. That creates suffering. I was devastated when my father died. From my perspective at the time, it was a shocking and agonising event. I had lost the only person I truly loved. But in the timeline of the universe, it was just business as usual. One form must transition to another.

'Everything is perfect' does not imply that everything and everybody is good. It simply means that all people are perfect the way they are. Perfect bastards and perfectly selfish people do exist. There are people who are perfectly ungrateful or perfectly mean. We have all met these types at some point in our lives. In my earlier years, I have hit the negative equivalent of a jackpot several times—meeting more than five of them in quick succession.

I don't know why I don't meet those types anymore. Maybe I don't notice them. Maybe I just don't give them any of my mind space. Maybe I've accepted the truth.

The truth is that everyone is merely a sum of his or her individual experiences. They have to be the way they are. They just can't help being themselves. They cannot be anyone else.

People read different books, have diverse friends, engage in myriad activities and have varied experiences. Therefore, they think and behave differently. I am just grateful to God for my own set of experiences.

If I had been born in a slum and my experiences had

been restricted to interactions with my neighbours there, I would be different from the person that I am today. If I had been born into a privileged family, there would have been a likelihood of my suffering from the privileged child syndrome. If I had gone through the same life experiences in the same sequence that any human being I detest had faced, it is probable that I could have been his ghostly double. I couldn't be anybody else with that exact set of experiences.

In my younger days, at the nadir of my life, I hated chaos but experienced lots of it. I had perfected the art of mismanaging relationships. I had this uncanny ability to destroy any relationship in a single interaction. As an asshole I'd score a perfect ten.

If any other human being on the planet had the same degree of insecurity and self-fixation, and had similar anger management issues, they too would be singing my songs of loneliness crammed with self-pitying lyrics. 'I'm stinging in the rain…Oh! I'm stinging in the rain.' What a waste.

Assume that chaos and suffering are wild weeds that I didn't want in my garden. But with my right hand while I was frantically plucking the weeds off the ground, with my left hand I was tossing the weed seeds back into the furrowed earth.

If everything is perfect, are we doomed? Quite the contrary. With deliberate actions of gratitude, kindness, compassion and an array of positive deeds, we can change our states into positive and happy ones. The more positivity we sow, the more positivity we reap. I have gone from being perfectly miserable to being perfectly happy. Anyone can.

One can generate good thoughts that will create good emotions and thereby ensure good actions. This can catapult one into a positive state of being. However, one can also begin by doing good actions. The actions will breed good emotions and soon translate into experiencing good thoughts.

Take your pick. Whether one begins with good actions or good thoughts, the end result is the same—one will become more perfectly positive and happy. This is a perfect formula. Even if you don't believe this, it's perfectly fine. For everything is perfect.

∽

• CHAPTER 2 •

NO CONDITIONS APPLY

WHAT IF A LIFESTYLE PRODUCT IS LAUNCHED WHICH guarantees that the buyer will definitely live a more enriched life? This is no scam or gimmick. It is a certainty. Obtaining this commodity will actually restructure the way you live and assure you of a positive change in all your relationships. The good relationships in your life will become better and the unpleasant ones will become healthy and wholesome.

And what if this product is distributed for free?

Assume that all the talk about its benefits are a hundred per cent true. Can you think of any commodity that people would refuse to buy despite its obvious benefits?

The product is happiness.

This is not a book that teaches you how to be happy or a list of dos and don'ts to be happy. There is no formula for happiness, neither does it contain any techniques or recipes.

Happiness is the product.

Since everyone wants to be happy, why do people refuse to buy it? Let me start the list with people in my world who turn away from happiness.

Daniella, a pre-teen, lost her father to cancer last week. Her happiness now lies in the future, when she finds a cure for the cursed disease.

Mr Shah, a diamond merchant, who was betrayed by his partner. He'd only buy happiness if he could morph it into a gun and shoot the bastard who swindled him.

Hannah, whose alcoholic husband is also a wife-beater,

would buy it only if it guaranteed a solution to her husband's alcoholism and its related problems.

Ricardo, whose son is being admitted for the nth time to a drug rehabilitation facility today, is simply not interested. He believes that happiness is just a fantasy and that no one in this world is or can be genuinely happy.

Robert has been unemployed for over a month. Offer him a job in a reputed company, and he'll take it any day over this thing called happiness.

Amirbhai, whose mortgages ensure just a hand-to-mouth existence. William the mechanic, who has a constantly irritable manager. Shilpa, a fresher in college, who has yet to make friends. Kevin, the boy who didn't get chosen for his school's football team.

Sammy, the heroin addict, who thinks, 'What can you do with happiness—shove it up your ass? Give me my poison. Will happiness remove the trauma of the past? Can it?'

It may be very obvious to you why the above-mentioned people will not buy the product. I wouldn't be surprised if only a tiny minority of the entire human population actually purchase or accept happiness.

Happiness, for most people, is conditional. Someone may want a home to be happy. On buying the home, realisation will dawn that not having a partner to share the home with will only mean desolation. A partner will fix it—so another condition is made, and happiness is postponed once again.

The companion might be satisfactory, or pathological. Assuming that the partner is a good person, what if the partner's needs cannot be met? Malaise and dejection again.

The conditions never cease. The wants? They go on and on and on.

Exactly like addicts who make drug use a condition to their happiness. 'Going to the Roger Waters concert will be mind-blowing, man. By the way, if you want me to be happy, just get me some weed, bro.'

Happiness is a choice. You don't have to buy happiness. In truth, there is no way you can buy it either.

You can simply choose to be happy. Really? Yes, really!

Even if pharmaceutical companies spend billions of dollars on research, they will never succeed in creating a happiness pill. It is not possible to create a chemical concoction for happiness—temporary euphoria, perhaps, but not happiness.

Of course, the anti-depressant industry is booming. But anti-depressants merely get you anti-depressed. An anti-depressed state of mind is not a depressed state of mind, but it is not a happy state of mind either.

You can choose to be happy on your way to acquiring a home, a spouse, a car, a child, or a fat bank balance. Though acquiring all of the above will not keep you happy anyway—newer wants will arise as your life keeps spiralling onward.

Happiness is not an outcome. It is a process.

My journey to happiness began as a child. When I asked my grandfather how I could be happy, he told me that happiness is merely the by-product of a good value system. He was right, but I was too young to make any sense of it. Now, I finally understand the wisdom in what he said.

It's easy to build a muscular body. That's just a result of regular workouts at the gym. If we work out regularly at the gym, we'll have the ripped body we want by default. Similarly, if we have a good set of values, we are bound to be happy.

Whenever I have compromised on a value, I've been unhappy.

In my younger days, I lied very often, both by telling untruths as well as by omission of facts. At a certain level I enjoyed lying. It shielded me from negative outcomes. On the flip side, lying always stressed me out. I had to constantly remember what lies I had told, when, to whom, and keep them straight. In addition, I disrespected myself and even when I got away with my lies, deep down I was unhappy.

I suffered from a sense of entitlement, and did not value gratitude. Much good came my way, but I barely saw it—I took all of it for granted. Revisiting those days, I recollect that I was too self-consumed, living in a bubble of self-pity—it added up to a state where I was grossly unhappy.

I even took my home for granted. I would bristle if my father entered my bedroom. It was only when we had an argument and I left his home that I realised my bedroom had always been within the boundaries of his home.

Until my thirties, the only rewards I sought were external—money, fame, appreciation, the approval of others, branded clothes, fancy toys, etc. Of course it was pleasurable but only in the moment. It was paradoxical: it ensured that happiness remained an ever elusive rainbow—you could see it, but it stayed forever in the distance. My decisions were based on the pleasure–discomfort axis. Actions were determined by the degree of pleasure I would perceive or the amount of discomfort I could circumvent.

When my first love, Veronica, unceremoniously dumped me, I was devastated. I attributed her leaving me to her absence of values. I thought she had rejected me because she preferred the-lad-with-the-dad-who-owned-a-Ferrari. But she had left me for other reasons: my extreme personality, the way in which I let my insecurity fuel my actions. Her values were fine. I was the one who didn't know what I truly valued.

I have to thank my father for shutting the doors of his home to me. Within a matter of weeks, I started actualising his discourses.

'I have lots of friends who care for me. I don't need you. If given a chance, they will look after my needs better than you do,' I had taunted him.

His response was gentle. He said, 'Fishes and guests stink after a few days, Bhai. I can only hope that you learn this soon.'

I understood the truth of what he'd said in the ten days after I left home. My friends—or those I'd considered my friends—treated me like putrid fish. Unwanted, my pride battered, I let my ego lead me to a life on the streets.

Left to fend for myself, I realised that my mastery of the blame game and the ability to guilt-trip others had worked wonderfully at home, but made survival much more difficult outside. My inability to delay gratification deepened my suffering.

Without a sense of commitment and hard work, I stood a zero chance at subsistence. I had to delete the 'mental' part of the 'sentimental' person that I had been. I had to bypass the emotional and impulsive decision-making that was my forte. I had to be practical in exercising choices and needed to outgrow my I-don't-want-to-be-a-grown-up syndrome.

I wasn't sure what my values were. But, slowly, I discovered what was important to me. When I decided that keeping my commitments was an important value, I started my journey back into the real world. I had only one real responsibility, a small one: I gave tuitions to Ankush Mehta. The Mehta family wouldn't have tolerated my coming late, so I forced myself to be on time, all the time. Then I decided that force wasn't necessary—I would make it a commitment to always be on time.

As the days passed by, I genuinely started to feel good. For perhaps the first time in my adult life, I began to truly respect myself for keeping my commitments. Ever since then, commitment has been a central value in my life.

On 26 July 2005, Mumbai was struck by a severe storm; the met department recorded more than three feet of rainfall in a single day. By then, it had been many years since I'd lived on the streets. I'd studied medicine, then stepped away from a career as a surgeon to a vocation that I could pour my heart into: setting up a rehabilitation centre where addicts could learn to recover and reclaim their lives. I had made a firm promise to myself on the day I set up Land, our rehabilitation centre in the Malanggad Valley outside Mumbai, that I would visit the centre every alternate day. 27 July was the scheduled day for my next visit.

It usually takes two hours from the main city to reach Land on a bad traffic day, but on that particular day it took more than seven hours, as the car crawled through stagnant water for most of the journey. To make matters worse, a part of the road had been washed away. So I had to proceed on foot.

When I finally reached Land's silver gates that day, I experienced an intense sense of happiness. I thought to myself, 'Doc doesn't break his promises.' The elation I felt was pure, undiluted bliss!

Values change so much in the span of a life. As a kid at home, I would literally fling a chapatti that was even slightly undercooked across the dining table—I was that demanding. The years I spent on the streets changed me. I was grateful for every morsel of anything that I put into my mouth. Surprisingly, the meals were more delectable and filling too. They tasted better for a reason: the special flavour came from my deep sense of gratitude.

'Values are subject to a test of inconvenience. The more inconvenienced you are while maintaining a value, the more you enjoy it,' my father had told me. I was experiencing his statement mathematically, as a law of direct proportionality between the variables, inconvenience and happiness. Values were the constant.

By the time I had graduated from medical college, a new

and sturdy set of values had blossomed in my life.Empathy, compassion, bravery, discipline, meaningful relationships and consistency were some of the values on which I would build a happy life for the next thirty years and more.

I genuinely value family now. Since many of my meaningful relationships had no biological connection but were family to me, I created my own definition of family: *Family is a unit that is created when people of common needs or interests or pursuits get together and share collectively, with mutual caring and respect.*

Today, I am proud to be a part of a wonderful family that includes my wife, kids, sister, and over 1200 recovering addicts and their families. This adds incredible value and happiness to my life.

Happiness = by-product of a good value system.

• CHAPTER 3 •

THE MEANING of LIFE

AND, JUST LIKE THAT, I FIGURED OUT THE MEANING OF LIFE. A mild current arced inwards from both shoulder blades. The two currents, which felt like thin lines of otherworldly electricity, merged at the top of my backbone and shot like a lightning bolt down my spine. I felt a sense of empowerment.

I had conducted a berserk search for 'the meaning of life' since my school days, much to my father's anguish. I didn't ask for permission to embark on these journeys—I would simply disappear from home for days together. My father's love for me surfaced as anger when I returned. He'd thrash me until he was exhausted. Then, he'd threaten me using several combinations of the words 'last', 'ultimate' and 'final' before throwing in the word 'warning'.

The threats always ended with him crying, 'Why are you torturing me?'

He knew I was disconnected from my mother, but he was not aware that I had caught her 'cheating' on him, as I thought at the time—nor did he know how that episode had impacted me. I truly felt abnormal, because my friends and everybody else seemed to be living in happy families.

We were different. All other mothers stayed at home with their children. Only my mother lived in another home. My father didn't understand my frustration, my angst, or my misery—and how could he? I had never shared it with him.

I often felt guilty. I knew he was suffering too, raising five kids as a single parent. He loved me dearly and I knew

Matter chose experience and became me. When i experience myself as one with the universe's consciousness, i can be whoever i want to be. May i be a channel of joy, connection and meaning to lives around me *

how much he cared for my well-being. I would promise never to repeat my erroneous ways again, and I always meant to keep that promise.

If selective amnesia is a disease, I had an extreme case of it. After a few months I would vanish again, completely forgetting the remorse I'd felt earlier.

I genuinely felt that everyone in the world should be a part of this mission, even my father. It bothered me that people were living pointless lives. They went around in the same circles day in and day out. Living automated lives. Suffering. Sacrificing. Cheating on one another. Playing mind games. Complying. Complaining. Chasing success. Mindlessly living each day.

From handcart pullers to pilots. From prostitutes to professors. From CEOs to con artists. All of them furiously committed to getting ahead of the pack. Unaware that the person who wins the race isn't going to live forever. Everyone seemed hypnotised by their own definition of survival, investing almost all their time and minds just to survive. I thought it was a great pity. People were living their lives just to die. Lives lived without any meaning. Such bullshit!

My journey to discover the meaning of life began on 13 September 1971 aboard the Dehradun Express. It was fuelled by the extra pocket money I'd received the day before, on my fifteenth birthday. My plan was simple. I'd board a train to Dehradun and engage co-passengers in solo conversations to gauge if they were intelligent enough. Then I would spring my question on them: 'What do you think is the meaning of life?'

I would restrict my interactions to older people who were travelling alone. Those who advertised their religion would give predictable answers and were eliminated from the word go.

After some thought, I zeroed in on a man chain-smoking

Charminar cigarettes. He seemed to be in his own zone, transfixed by something outside the moving train. His face was riddled with pain. He didn't notice me settle into the empty seat across his.

'Good evening. Do you have more cigarettes?' I inquired with a smile, nodding towards his shirt pocket where the Charminar pack was outlined.

'*Gando che? Besharam!* You are a child. Aren't you ashamed to ask me for a cigarette? They are bad for you,' he said.

He reminded me of my father. He, too, had one set of rules for himself and another for us children. When I had slapped a classmate who was bullying someone from a junior class, my dad reminded me that it was the wrong thing to do. However, if he beat me up, there was always a 'good' reason to justify the action. It was for my good. He was guided by the golden rule of those years: 'Spare the rod and spoil the child'. Little did he realise that I had my own set of rules. One of them was: 'Use the rod and lose the child'.

If I was dishonest, it meant that I was a liar. I had no values and my father would punish me for not telling the truth. But the rules were different for him. When I told callers on the phone, at his behest, that he was not at home, that was not fraudulent behaviour.

This gentleman on the train was another such person who had double standards.

My 'I'm-so-misunderstood' expression almost always got me out of trouble at school and with strangers. I would slightly tilt my neck to one side, squeeze my nose and forehead upwards, and raise my left eyebrow a little higher. It was like a well-rehearsed magic trick that always had the desired effect.

I put on the sham: 'Sorry, Uncle, you misunderstood me. I don't smoke. I saw you puffing non-stop and that's why I was hoping you didn't have any more cigarettes.'

Placing my right thumb on my chin with the right index finger covering my upper lip to resemble a moustache, I added, assertively, 'Uncle, cigarette smoking causes cancer. Please don't smoke so much.'

He smiled. I'd hit the bullseye.

What followed was a long-drawn-out monologue that began with the bad monsoon responsible for the crop failure in his village, Boidara. He spoke of the corrupt politicians siphoning off funds, the tyranny of moneylenders and many other subjects which were irrelevant to my forthcoming question. Finally, the speech ended with his visit to Mumbai to see a doctor for the severe pain and swelling in both his knees. Ah-thai-tis, he called it, slanting his eyebrows upward and slowly bobbing his head from side to side.

'What did the doctor say? He gave you medicines? Don't worry, you will be fine soon,' I said, trying to put him at ease.

He started another speech stating that there was no cure for his arthritis, for which he would have to take medicines for the rest of his life.

Inadvertently, he was answering my question. 'I'm just paying for the sins of my last birth. This is karma. I have suffered so much. The rest of my life will go on like this. When I have paid for all my sins, I will be born again in good circumstances and then I will attain moksha. Then I will never be born again.'

That didn't make any sense. The cosmic math was all fucked up. The following thoughts flooded my mind: Assuming we would all commit some sins in this life, even if we level out those sins from the past birth, we would have to be born again to atone for the sins accumulated in this lifetime. If $x = y + z$ and all you can level out is the y of the equation, the remainder z ensures that you are born again.

If the meaning of life is not to be born again, then why were we born in the first place? Just so that we are not going to be born again? That's quite ridiculous.

I knew this old man merely used this philosophy to live as happily as he could. In the hope that in his next birth he might be born into some royal family. 'Live for another day' is understandable. But 'live for another life'? No way. What if there isn't another life? What if your karma is good but you are born again as a tadpole? You get an extra pink dot on the back of your hand. That's it?

In order not to disturb his peace of mind, I decided to keep my inferences to myself and changed the topic.

'Will you please wake me up in the morning?' I asked, yawning and pretending to look sleepy.

'I'll be getting off at Ankleshwar at 4 a.m. Didn't you say you are going to Dehradun? This train takes forty-one hours to get there. Two full days and nights. What's the rush to wake up? Goodnight.'

1600 kilometres in 41 hours. I did the math. We were going to be travelling 'expressly' at about 39 kilometres per hour. That's not even twice as fast as a horse. Whoever christened this snail train Dehradun Express either had a poor knowledge of English or a rich sense of humour.

Climbing onto my designated sleeper berth on the top, I tore open a packet of milk biscuits and wolfed them down. I made a pillow by folding my bedsheet over my backpack. The conversations of fellow passengers soon quietened and merged with the monotonous clickety-clack thadak-thadak of the train rumbling through the night.

My low boredom threshold, the continual stench from the latrine six feet away, and the absurd explanation to my question—those were enough to make me call off my trip at Nizamuddin Station in Delhi, half a day before the scheduled destination.

Since then I've made many more journeys, and heard various ridiculous theories. I rejected all of them outright. My question was sincere, but it would almost always turn into an ego trip, an argument that had to be won.

Once, an elderly lady belted out the God–Devil, Good–Bad and Heaven–Hell concept. Our discussion led us to a stage where I requested she define the word 'good'. When she responded by defining good as 'not harming others', I politely informed her that in the last two minutes of our discussion she had not only harmed but killed millions of bacteria.

Taken aback at first, she recovered quickly: 'Son, you can't see bacteria.' Though I fully understood what she was trying to say, I had to win the argument. I assumed an expression of innocent curiosity. 'If I shoot someone far away with a rifle, and I don't see him harmed, would it fall within your definition of "good"?' I asked.

'You will grow into a murderer,' the lady said, exasperated.

The conversation ended abruptly.

On another occasion, a gentleman explained to me his concept of God. 'You cannot see God,' he declared as he stood up, flicking on the switch of the compartment's ceiling fan. He threw his hands up dramatically. 'You saw the fan come on, but did you see the electricity?'

Before I could react to the question, he concluded his theatrical performance with a flourish, 'You cannot see God, but he exists.'

His stagecraft annoyed me as much as his ideology. I suppressed my annoyance, thanked him, and then motioned for him to sit beside me on the berth. I requested him to look deeply into my eyes. Our gazes locked for a few seconds and then I asked him, punctuating every word with a pause, 'Can you see a huge red ball with blue stripes floating in the air between us?'

He moved away from me: 'Why are you asking me this question?'

I said that if his logic about electricity was correct, then there should also be a red ball with blue stripes. We can't see either of them, therefore, both must exist.

He leapt to his feet and told me that the Devil had touched me and that I should beg for God's forgiveness. I told him what I thought of the Devil. The Devil was just a fantasy. The Devil was merely a scapegoat for those who sinned. People sinned out of choice and then blamed it on the Devil.

I told him that he was crazy to believe that all humans are angels and the sins they commit are solely because the Devil influences them.

He snarled, 'Your mind has been taken over by the Devil!'

After several train journeys and dozens of similarly mindless interactions, I came to a conclusion. There had to be another way to get my question answered. The common denominators in most of the theories were distorted concepts of God. I truly believe in God, but I didn't buy any of the ideas of God these people shared with me.

The God of my understanding is omnipresent, and all-knowing. Possessing infinite love, compassion and wisdom beyond human comprehension. This God of my understanding cannot create a hell with oceans of fire with numerous snakes and scorpions to torture his creations. Even if I shut my brain off to try to buy into this theory, I still cannot comprehend why the snakes and scorpions in the fire would not be broiled themselves.

I believe that both Heaven and Hell happen on earth. We live through them in our lifetime. Heaven and Hell are just different states of mind.

When we do good, what we feel is heaven—and vice-versa. There are no rewards or penalties in the afterlife.

The laws of cause and effect are equal and simultaneous. However, to be cognisant of the synchronicity might take a long time on most occasions. Even if there is an afterlife, it would be governed by the same laws as our present universe.

God shaped Creation and then held Creation with laws that were uniformly applicable to the whole of it.

This concept made sense to me though it still didn't answer my question, 'What is the meaning of life?'

Many futile voyages and dissatisfying responses later, I found myself at The Theosophical Society campus in Adyar, Chennai. It's a beautiful two-hundred-acre property on the southern bank of the Adyar River. Sitting under the magnificent banyan tree that spread over four acres, I was enveloped by a field of positive energy. I have read somewhere that an average banyan tree has the cooling capacity of a 200 tonne air-conditioning plant. It must be true, for it was definitely a few degrees cooler here than at the beach about a hundred metres away.

A senior citizen emerged from the Adyar Library and Research Centre nearby. She was ambling in my direction carrying a pile of books. She could be a good candidate.

I got up and approached her with a smile. She returned my smile affectionately.

Something within me already knew that she had the answer. The excitement made me forget my strategy to begin with small talk first. 'Good evening, ma'am. Can you tell me what the meaning of life is?' I got right to the question.

Placing her right palm over my head she said, 'How old are you, son?'

I responded instantly, 'Nineteen-and-a-half.'

She crinkled her eyes and laughed. 'Now you are adding "and a half" to your age. Trust me, as you grow older you will stop adding "and a half". Later, you'll be omitting real numbers. You'll refer to your age in approximations like mid-thirties or early forties.'

She smiled at me. 'I am in my early sixties. Son, forget this intellectual question. I can assure you from my experience that every subsequent birthday comes faster. Just enjoy every moment that you are alive. Try to leave a trail of joy wherever you go.'

She ruffled my hair affectionately and carried on walking.

My calculations confirmed her advice. The nineteenth year of my life would take 1/19 or .05 per cent of the total life that I had experienced till then. In the sixtieth year of my life, my perception of time would alter dramatically to a mere .01 per cent of my life. It means that the days will appear to pass by five times faster.

I took a slow, deep breath with the intention of enjoying the process of breathing. Whoooosh! For the next fifteen minutes I was fixated to a point on an aerial root about a foot above the ground. I focussed on my breathing, maintaining the intent. The aesthetic qualities of the aerial root came alive and engrossed my consciousness. There was no sense of 'I'. All that was left was love.

I do not have the potential, the talent or the time to describe even in a million words the sense of joy that I experienced then. What the Mughal emperor Jehangir said as he set his eyes on the Valley of Kashmir describes an infinitesimal fraction of the vast love that I felt. 'If there is paradise upon earth, it is here.'

I went to our dormitory near Blavatsky Lodge. Ankush Mehta, the friend who was responsible for this break-a-tion (break from life), was lying on a mattress on the floor. He looked at me oddly and said, 'The Theosophical Society (T.S.) does not permit smoking on campus. You look blown, man. If my mom finds out, I'm screwed.'

'Ankush, you know drugs are not my scene,' I said. Then I told him, tripping over my words in excitement, of my encounter with the lady and the aerial root. He chuckled disbelievingly, still thinking that I was 'tripping'. He was right. I was 'tripping'. On life.

This was a beautiful experience but the answer to my question still evaded me: 'What is the meaning of life?'

The answer came at night. I was sitting alone on a private beach at the T.S. trying my best to get rid of psychological time and to live in the moment. The ocean's waves broke over the beach; the tide ebbed and returned. The water's ebb and flow was tranquilising, the ocean's gentle sounds held me in a trance.

My reverie was interrupted by a gentleman with a flowing beard. He was walking towards me from the shoreline. He sat down beside me on the sand and extended his right hand. 'Hi! I'm Maitreya.'

'I'm Yusuf. Friends call me Bhai.' I smiled, shaking hands with him.

He inquired if I had come to attend the annual convention. I said no, and informed him that I'd come to find the meaning of life.

'What life?' he asked.

I reframed my question, thinking that he didn't understand it. I put on a serious expression, 'What is the meaning of life, umm…what is the meaning of existence?'

'What existence?' Maitreya asked promptly.

My ego got injured; I assumed he was being sarcastic. The honesty behind my question was lost and I was on an ego trip once again. Battle lines were drawn in my mind. Whatever happened now, I had to win.

After some contemplation, a battle plan was chalked out. I had to instigate him to talk about the cycle of karma. And I had a question ready for that. Even higher exponents of Hindu philosophy have not been able to answer that question.

I shot a questioning look at him and began, 'Are you a believer in the *shunya* (nothingness) theory?'

'Yes,' he replied.

Certain that he was falling into my trap, I moved a little closer to him and asserted, 'You believe that nothing exists. So you don't exist. I don't exist. Nothing exists. Therefore, you presume that this question also doesn't exist.'

He smiled back. 'Precisely.'

I had expected a strong reaction to my statement. Instead of the predicted negativity, his smile conveyed a different message.

He touched my left shoulder lightly and said, his voice clear and kind, 'Bhai, have you ever had a dream?'

'Yes,' I said.

'Have you seen trees in your dream?' he inquired.

I closed my eyes and scanned my memory. I tried hard to remember if there were trees in any of my dreams. I didn't recall any. Then, in a flash, I recalled a recent dream: I saw myself floating amongst clouds.

I replied excitedly, 'I don't remember seeing trees, but I remember seeing clouds.'

'Were they real?'

'No,' I said.

Feigning seriousness, I returned to my plan, baiting him to my trap with a question. If he answered in the affirmative, I won. From that position, it was checkmate. I asked if he believed in karma. He did.

It was the right time to rattle his nerves. I unleashed my next question. 'It means I am born in this birth for the sins in my last birth. Is that correct?'

He nodded, yes.

Charged, sensing a thumping victory, I carried on with the unanswerable question, 'I took on a life form in my earlier birth for the sins of the life before that and so on. But there must've been a point in time when there was zero karma. So why did I come into being in the first instance?'

He was not perturbed by my question at all. His eyes softened into a warm smile. 'That's because it is the nature of matter to seek experience. Do you understand?'

I could sense his intentions now—genial, benign, they compelled me to abandon my ego trip. I did not want to win the argument anymore. I wanted to know. I wanted to learn. I wanted to interpret what he was trying to explain to me.

'Bhai, everything is in a state of "what is" and "what is not". Are you familiar with electrons? You know these electrons cannot be in one place. They are constantly changing positions.'

He sketched the electron's path in the air with his hands, punctuating every word with momentary crane beaks with his fingers and thumb coming to a point, 'Electrons are in different places all the time.'

He kept repeating the crane beak action over and over with the words…what is…what is not…what is…what is not.

Even though I didn't understand him entirely, I loved the answer because it involved my first love: physics.

Physics offered me solace during my traumatic childhood. All human beings were too variable. Everyone behaved in unpredictable ways all the time. I needed constants to comfort me. Physics provided those constants. Physics made me experience equality not only with my dad and mom, but with all living beings. It didn't matter who they were, but if a person jumped from a height, they would only travel towards the ground at 32ft/sec irrespective of age, class or creed.

The rules were uniform.

I closed my eyes and visualised electrons moving in orbits around an atom. They could not be in the same place. I told him that I agreed that nothing was static and nothing could be.

He continued, 'So when matter, at random, chooses life form as an experience, it gets bonded with the karma cycle.'

I did not fully grasp the theory he propounded about the randomness of life, but I knew in my heart that he was making sense. Keeping it simple, I revisited the 'what's life?' part of the conversation in my mind. Looking away from my friend, I turned towards the sea. I zoned out under the moonlight and delved into another surreal 'aerial root' experience.

I saw thoughts transforming into clouds. After a while, the clouds merged into a flash of nothingness. Eureka!

Overwhelmed by the spiritual experience, I turned towards Maitreya and said, 'If we assume there is no life, then there is no meaning to life. Which means we can choose to give our life any meaning. We have the power to choose our own meaning. Wow!'

Maitreya smiled in agreement.

I felt excited and empowered by the discovery. Deliberating over several choices, I'd finally deciphered the meaning of my life. It was to enrich the life of at least one other human being. That was my purpose.

I could choose any meaning that I wanted for my relationships, my family, for love, for friendship, for the process of ageing, for every damn thing.

I felt empowered.

• CHAPTER 4 •

The Magic of Imagination

IT FELT LIKE A RAT LIVED INSIDE MY STOMACH. ONCE IN a while, it lunged at me (or so I imagined), squeezing a bit of my flesh with its four front teeth. Holding the bite, while shaking its head violently. Struggling to separate the meat caught between its teeth. Backing off. Then repeating the routine. Over and over. Until then, I'd believed that only the absence of love hurt. Being hungry for six days hurt more.

Even though I was drinking copious amounts of water to dilute the pain, it didn't help. Not even slightly. Later, when I was at medical school, I learnt that no amount of water could have changed the PH (acidity) levels in my stomach.

My mental energies were severely depleted too. I didn't have the bandwidth to deal with reality anymore. I could probably walk back home, apologise to my father, and return to living a life of luxury. That was only a probability, not a possibility. I would rather have died than weasel back to him. I decided to stop living.

In retrospect, the suicide attempts feel almost comical. My decision to walk into the sea was preceded by a longish bitchy monologue cursing God. The attempt lasted less than three seconds after I stepped into the water. It was freezing cold. I wanted to die, quickly, in peace. Freezing to death slowly wasn't an option.

As I walked towards the main road from the beach, I saw water tankers zipping by. I could surprise the next truck's driver with a hurricane appearance in front of his bumper. I could see my body crushed underneath his vehicle. This attempt lasted much longer than the 'freezing in the sea' option. Ten seconds.

Before I could even contemplate celebrating my death by being run over by a truck, a thought struck me. What if he swerved and broke only my lower limbs? I would be wheel-chaired from the hospital straight to my father's home. WTF!

Trudging back dejectedly to the Mumbai Central S.T. depot, I slumped into my favourite sleeping spot. 'You can't even kill yourself, what kind of a loser are you?' echoed a voice in my head. This was the first failure where I could not pin the blame on either of my parents. Or anyone else. For every failure before this, I invariably blamed them. There was a scapegoat. Always.

Not this time. I couldn't kill myself simply because I didn't have the balls. I was a coward. That was the lowest point of my life.

By now, the rat that lived in my stomach seemed to have invited friends and family over. I had to eat. It was 5 a.m. Coolies and porters vied with each other for customers as buses drew up and passengers arrived at the depot. I had to shatter either my resolve to survive—or my ego. Choosing to break the latter, I approached the next bus entering the depot, feigning the confidence of a veteran porter and earnestly attempting to mimic their body language.

I bent and picked up two random suitcases that had been tossed out of the luggage hold. Before I could spot the owner, I was pushed so hard that I fell to the pavement. '*Saala*, those are my bags. Keep your filthy hands off them. *Chalo!*' The man shouting at me was dressed in white, sporting the kind of jewellery worn by aspiring gangsters in Mumbai.

I limped back slowly to my sleeping spot, about ten yards away. Scared, bruised, angry, and hungry. The pain of rejection added to the overwhelming hunger pangs. I cried for a long time.

'How does one survive without any help?'

'Is it even possible for anyone to make it on their own?'

'Why does life have to be so cruel?'

Negative questions like these consumed my brain, consuming me. Then, out of the blue, a thought struck me: *'Suppose I make it?'*

If I made it, what an achievement it would be! Without any help, without anyone by my side, if I could carve out a space for myself in this 'cruel' world, then I'd be making it on my own. Suppose it really happened? Wow!

For the next half an hour or so, I was engrossed in dreaming up detailed images of my future. Visualising the goals and the dreams I wanted to fulfil, down to the last detail. I carefully planned my financial independence. I imagined what it would feel like to have a loving family, a beautiful home. I imagined a time when I'd become an institution. I could see a time ahead when I was adding meaning to countless lives. I was respected, for being me. I was a self-made man.

The super abundant visuals filled me with joy. I knew it was going to happen once it had already happened in my mind. Years ago, my father had told me, 'Bhai, whatever happens, happens twice. First in your mind and then in your reality. Success, failure, friendships, actually everything!'

I was fired up, the hunger and the exhaustion now forgotten. The time period didn't matter at all. I was confident of the beautiful eventuality. The positive feelings I'd conjured up with my thoughts revitalised me. I was cocooned by a positive force—a beautiful butterfly dancing for abundant nectar.

A few futile attempts later, I finally managed to help an elderly couple transport their luggage to a taxi outside the bus depot. Their generous coins were sufficient to send the rats packing. The eight biscuits that their tip fetched me, downed with the free water available, banished the hunger. Thankfully, I've never felt the rats again.

Within a few weeks, I'd grown better at earning a few rupees. I would size up the body language of the disembarking passengers within seconds and zero in on my target. Tadaa!

As soon as I had the chance to be a tutor, I quit my erstwhile career as a coolie. Time swallowed the six long years it took me to become a doctor. It didn't matter—I had no doubt that I would create history, create an institution that would change lives, and make this world a better place. At least a dozen person at a time.

By 1985, I had made a start as a doctor with an interest in drug rehabilitation. Menka Shivdasani, a journalist from *The Afternoon Despatch and Courier*, came to interview me about the state of addiction in Mumbai. 'Where do you see yourself ten years from now?' she asked. She published my response three days later in the paper.

But I had no time to think about newspaper interviews. My patients kept me busy. They stayed with me at my residence, and I spent hours learning and unlearning with, and from, them. Rehabilitation was not a career—it was my life.

My patients provided me with a fluid family. The faces changed every year, but the togetherness, the sharing and the comradeship were constant. The feeling of family was strong and continuous.

In 1995, I invested my savings and bought about two acres of barren land on the outskirts of Kalyan city, near Mumbai. Standing in the scorching heat out on the rocks, with only the lizards and birds for company, I pictured in my mind the physical reality of the institution as powerfully as I could.

There would be plenty of leafy trees forming a canopy alongside the stone flags of the winding pathway. They would shield the patients from the sun. There'd be boarding houses for the patients, spaced a little apart from each other. A club house for indoor games, a small court for outdoor games like badminton and football. I could also envisage a little open space sufficient for a modest gymnasium.

In everybody else's mind, I was just a doctor who lived with a dozen patients at home. I never saw it like that. I was an institution. I was living it.

A few years earlier, I had virtually been living in Fiat taxis, treating drug dependents and depressives all over Mumbai. The traffic and distances didn't bother me. I knew that I was going to be an institution in other people's realities too, soon. In my mind, I already was.

As I grew into a bigger institution, I didn't know what challenges lay ahead. But I was pretty sure that there would be tough and busy days. I was grateful to God for the match practice.

Sometime in early 2009, I was sharing stories of my life with my twelve-year-old daughter. 'Bliss, I was a celebrity when you were younger. I've opted out of that shit. First, because it's only an illusion. Second, because I've seen that the press is only interested in increasing its circulation. They turn ordinary guys like me into celebrities. It has a two-fold benefit. They sell their papers while they are turning people into celebs. Then they sell larger volumes when they are bringing the celebs down. I think our generation loves to witness great falls. I'm not going to be their Humpty Dumpty.'

'Papa, do you have any photograph or press clipping

from your celebrity days?' she asked me excitedly. I pulled out a bunch that the office had spiral-bound and saved from the late 1980s.

As she flipped through them, I enjoyed observing her reactions. I always do. This time, it was more refreshing. Joy and pride radiated from her face. She was almost bouncing with excitement. 'Omg! Papa, this is too cool,' she smiled exuberantly. Then she stopped, holding out a file.

'Hey, what's this? You described Land, your rehab centre, way back in 1985. That was ten years before I was born. Read this!' She pointed to a paragraph in Menka's article in the *Afternoon* newspaper from 12 May 1985.

'While he currently treats them at his residence, Dr Merchant is planning a mini-village complex for rehabilitation of drug addicts...near Thane. The village will have a detoxification centre for 30 addicts at a time. Recreation facilities include a sports field, a conference room for prayer and sharing, and a day care centre. Pursuits like gardening and fine arts will be encouraged.'

I grabbed the file, stunned. I had genuinely forgotten about the interview. It was an exact description of the rehab facility in its current physical form. Even the number of patients mentioned in the article was the same as the number we currently accommodated.

How could that be possible? I hadn't even been aware of the steps I was taking towards that reality. I was genuinely surprised. All I can remember is that when Bliss turned nine months old, I'd confided, sadly, to my wife Sangita: 'The rehab has to be shifted out of our home if Bliss is to have a normal life.' I realised that it might affect the recovery process of the patients, but I was going to do it. Bliss deserved a normal upbringing.

Incidentally, the success rate increased. The moment I was less freely available to the patients, the more they valued the time I spent with them. Together, we developed a model where the patients had high degrees of independence and autonomy in the rehab while remaining under supervision and constant care.

I can, without doubt, conclude the following: it was the power of positive visualisation combined with fully feeling and experiencing the end result and wholly picturing those dreams that created the reality. It was a combination of my intentions, the positive visualisations and the required actions that spun the magic wand, thereby creating a magic land that has healed hundreds of depressives and drug dependents.

A land where love and recovery go hand-in-hand, and gratitude runs like a stream.

∾

II. MIND GAMES

the fundamentals

• CHAPTER 5 •

The AMBULANCE FUNDA

WHEN AN ADDICT OR AN ALCOHOLIC SUCCESSFULLY completes the rehabilitation programme at my centre, I never get carried away by the praise their loved ones lavish upon me. I am mindful of the fact that they are responding to their idea of me, the by-line that they are painting on me. To them, in that moment, I am neither 'Bhai' nor 'Doc', but 'the man who saved my child'.

Every time we interact with somebody, we are not only relating to who they are, but also to the imaginary by-lines we cast over them.

I know a guy—let's call him Steve—whose story I'll tell here to illustrate my point.

Steve loved Sundays. There was a rhythm to his Sunday evenings. His car, a sleek Nissan Terrano, would be waiting in the porch outside. Two bodyguards, burly and dressed in sharp suits, would escort him right to the door. One of them would put on his chauffeur's cap and get behind the wheel (a careful eye might have spotted the almost invisible bulge made by his Sig Sauer P229 handgun). The other always made sure that Steve was comfortably settled in the back before he got in beside him.

Pizza Hut was their usual stop. One of the guards would order the pizza, first checking with Steve which toppings he would like. The other guard always jumped out, casting a careful eye over the street and making sure that he was near Steve at all times, though he was unobtrusive about it.

Steve liked the fifteen minutes of solitude when the bodyguards waited to collect their pizza. He enjoyed watching the teenagers hanging out at the mall. Every so often, he would notice them staring at him quite openly. Sometimes, they'd smile at him. It happened every time, and he soaked in the attention as the kids looked at the well-dressed man in the fancy car. When they whispered to one another, he felt like a mini-celebrity. He wondered what they were saying.

'They probably think I'm a big shot, with bodyguards waiting on me hand and foot,' Steve would say to himself. Sometimes he would catch one of the kids staring at him, and he'd raise his hand slightly, waving in benevolent acknowledgement.

Steve started to love these Sunday outings. They were a relief from the daily grind, the tyranny of his normal routine back at the big house. And the attention that the kids showered on him when he visited Pizza Hut made him feel young again, powerful, attractive, someone who commanded attention. His troubles and worries receded from his mind. 'I feel like a rock star!' he thought to himself.

It took a little negotiating, but Steve managed to convince his team at the big house to let him get out of the Terrano and order his own pizza. He could do that on the next Pizza Hut visit, they said, but on one condition: both his bodyguards would accompany him to the counter.

All through the week, Steve waited impatiently for Sunday to arrive. That afternoon, he took out his favourite suit, an Armani, which he hadn't worn in a long while. He selected an Hermes tie and a pair of Italian loafers.

When he stepped out of the Terrano, he saw people turning to look at him, and he smiled inwardly at the surprise on their faces. Steve's walk took on a slightly confident strut. 'Wow!' he thought. 'These people must think I'm seriously important, some big shit walking around with these two bodyguards.'

As he stood in line waiting for his pizza, a pretty girl seated at a table across smiled at him. 'How're you doing?' she asked kindly. He nodded back, offering a modest smile and flashing the thumbs-up sign. At the tables ahead, a few more teenagers smiled at him. One or two even waved.

'So this is what it feels like to be a big shot!' Steve thought. He could get used to this—he felt like he was floating on cloud nine, while the pizza arrived. His bodyguard carried the box for him, and Steve turned around to get back into the car.

He froze, his expression changing. He'd never looked at the other side of the Nissan Terrano before. The driver's side was painted silver. A large logo on the other side now caught and held his eye. A sign announced in bold, black lettering across the paint: The Sunshine Rehab Centre and Psychiatric Institute: Home for the Mentally Challenged.

Steve had almost begun to believe that he really was a celebrity. He'd neglected the fact that he'd been admitted to the Sunshine Rehab Centre despite his protests, after his family and employers had confronted him with the fact that his alcoholism had turned him into a basket case. He'd thought that the kids at Pizza Hut were impressed with his mini-celebrity status. But they'd been whispering and staring because they saw him as a patient from a rehab centre, a mentally challenged person, possibly a psychopath! Waves of embarrassment washed over him. But the sign also confronted him with the truth. He could no longer hide behind a false mask.

I've seen people in Steve's situation very often. Any man arriving at Pattaya's infamous Walking Street in Thailand experiences an immediate status upgrade. The street is peppered with Thai and Russian commercial sex workers, vying for the attention of all the men passing by. And as the men puff up their chests and bring out their best smiles, the sex workers blush, giggle, and pretend to be charmed.

How many of these men realise that the sex workers are simply responding to a single word, a by-line written in invisible ink on their bodies? Money!

Singular by-lines are painted on a mass scale too. At sporting events, the colours of jerseys make us view those wearing our colours as 'us' and those wearing the opposition's colours as 'them'. During riots too, 'us' and 'them' by-lines are painted on people, polarised by religion, caste, colour or class.

In William Golding's *Lord of the Flies*, Jack's relentless chant 'Kill the Pig' makes it easier for the group to contemplate a terrible act—the by-line substitutes 'one of us' with a strange, non-human entity, 'the Pig'.

Hitler's Nazis painted 'rats' and the yellow Star of David as by-lines on Jews, in order to make it easier to slaughter them. It would have been psychologically impossible for the Germans to inflict such terrible atrocities without dehumanising the Jews first. Would any German have been as brutal if Hitler had commanded: 'Those human beings, who are just like you and me, should be slaughtered mercilessly'?

People are painting different by-lines on your 'ambulance', your imagined perception of yourself, at different points in time—be mindful of that. Being mindful will help you to not react to them. You can choose how to respond without being hurt or flattered.

A good by-line to write on people's 'ambulances' is Love.

Just imagine how beautiful one would feel if one could

write and see the by-line 'Love' on all the people one interacts with. Even if one per cent of the human population engaged with each other with love, the future painted in John Lennon's song *'Imagine'* would surely become the truth, some day.

CHAPTER 6

THE TRAIN STATION

AT LAND, WE HAVE A TRADITION THAT'S GROWN OVER the years. Every person who completes the rehabilitation programme successfully is thrown a farewell party. It's a beautiful celebration—other members of the programme share their memories, dress up in their best clothes, decorate the Therapy Hall with bright streamers and hand-drawn cards, and there's plenty of laughter.

In the time that they've spent at Land, most participants travel a great emotional distance, discovering truths about themselves, finding a new love for life and, often, a new sense of purpose. Frequently, those who are new to the programme, still caught up in traumas from the old addict's life that they are in the process of leaving behind, would have their first glimpse of a life of hope, possibility and joy at someone's farewell. These are special occasions, and most programmers leave on a wave of beautiful memories, goodwill and benedictions.

Ex-participants often return to Land, sometimes many years after they've sorted themselves out. They are always welcome, though we leave it up to those who've graduated to decide on how often they want to come back.

Some visit once a year, spending a few nights at Land, walking from the silver gates to the lawn outside, sharing their experiences and their lives after the programme with the new batch of people, who listen against the background of the green, gently sloping mountains of Haji Malang

People and events have passed, circumstances and connections will come. As my journey hurtles relentlessly on, i am fully present here and now, undistractedly living this ephemeral moment with you ✽

in the distance. Some come back with their children and their families after twenty years. A few drop in whenever they're in Mumbai. Often, it's the participants' families who stay in touch—one sent large tins of biscuits as a token of gratitude for a whole year after he'd left Land. To me, every one of them is special.

One week, we were making plans for Nabeel's farewell when another member, Arpita, asked, 'Do you think we'll stay in touch with each other, or will we leave and forget about one another?'

Nabeel must have been thinking along the same lines. He said, 'Does it matter so much? Maybe what's really important is that we shared part of our journey together.'

'What do you think?' Arpita asked me. 'Is that enough, Doc?'

'One of my friends was a train conductor,' I said. 'He was a bit of a character, Jim Baxter—a fabulous trumpet player in his spare time, but he spent most of his life on trains. When he retired, he told me, "Yusuf, you know what? All human beings live in a train compartment all their lives."'

I was thinking of Jim, his broad, kindly face suddenly solemn when he told me this. He'd said, 'It's true. When we are born, the train compartment commences its journey. All our trains are headed towards the same destination: Death. That's the final stop for everyone. This is not bollocks, mate. Give it a think.'

'What he meant,' I explained, 'was that no one can really escape the compartment called Life. When someone enters your field of vision, they enter your compartment. The first people who entered mine were probably my mother, the doctor and a few nurses. The doctor and the nurses faded—in Jim's terms, they left my compartment and I've never seen them since. I don't recollect their faces.

'Occasionally, I would see blurred funny faces making

gibberish sounds above me. Adults think babies are dumb, but some of us remember those early days very distinctly. Those adults really weren't important, as they hopped out of my field of vision before I could really get to know them or make any sense of their presence.

'My first day at school, I saw many new co-passengers. They were all of my age, except for the teacher. They would spend a few hours in my train before they stepped off. Then, unfailingly, they would reappear again the next day. Whenever they stepped out, my mother would step back into the train.

'Year after year, the co-passengers were substituted frequently. People would come and go. I was the only constant in the train. Some left and returned later, some never did return.'

Nabeel frowned, but Arpita said, 'That makes sense. When my father died, I was just six. I didn't know what death was—from my perspective, he left me and never came back again. My mom told me that he had gone to God's home. I understand what your friend means when he says life's like a train compartment. I spent the next three years waiting for my dad to come back again, waiting near the door of my train compartment. From the time I was six to the year I turned nine, I missed my dad so much that I paid no attention to the others who were in my life's train.'

'If it helps, that's an experience you have in common with others,' I said. 'In my younger years, I felt that I'd been waiting near the exit door of my own life's compartment, most of the time. I wasn't enjoying the company of the people in my compartment back then.'

Nabeel said, 'Why not?'

'Because I'd been waiting for some memories—most of them troubled ones—to leave my reality. Or, I was waiting for the wrong person, or I was waiting for good times from the past to reappear. Jim would have said that while I was waiting at the exit, the train was chugging towards its end in any case. Everything changed when I realised that I was just wasting my time—it was the present that mattered most.'

Nabeel laughed as realisation dawned upon him, 'Yeah! I'd spent so much time waiting for some casual girlfriend to come along, or for the pusher to deliver drugs, or something totally random. But I don't feel that way anymore, strangely enough. I'm not waiting for anything these days; I'm just happy to be here, doing whatever I'm supposed to be doing in the moment.'

Nabeel had changed so much over the course of the programme. He'd gone from being a sad, closed boy, suspicious of everyone else, to being an open, expansive, quietly impressive man, a good friend to many in his batch.

'You've got it!' I said to Nabeel. He grinned, but now Arpita seemed confused, so I explained.

'The trick is to enjoy with whoever is in the compartment,' I said. 'If you prefer, you can wait at the door and squander your time. The train will not wait; it will keep rumbling on.'

Nabeel said to Arpita, 'I think I get it. There was a time when my mother, my father, my sister and my friends were around—but they were in a far corner of my life's train. I probably gave my dog, Typo, more attention than I gave them. I spent my time sulking, or partying, or I was out drinking with my mates when I could have hung out with my family.'

'You seemed pretty happy on your last trip home,' she said. 'Your sister wanted to watch that daft Bollywood film and you were so cool with it.'

'Yeah, I guess because it wasn't the film that mattered so much—it was spending time with her,' Nabeel said.

I listened to them talking about their families, their

friends, their plans for the future, and I knew they'd both got it. Some of my friends from college hadn't been as lucky as these two young adults. They'd spent their lives mired in property squabbles, or had been so preoccupied with pressures of business that they missed out on their children growing up. Other friends, and many of the programmers who'd left Land, had figured it out.

All of us are on the same train. It's speeding towards death—the years go by faster than any of us realise. Just the other day, for instance, one of Land's first programmers, Jamshed, had flown to Mumbai from Zurich for a visit. He'd been twenty-two when we bid him farewell. Now he's a happy, prosperous green technology entrepreneur in his fifties, with two lovely kids and a warm-hearted, elegant wife. Time rushes by.

Our families are on the same train. We could make the short time we have together difficult, with obstacles and fights, or we could make their voyage in our life's train compartment as beautiful as we can. Because we can! Why waste the years?

The night sky was soft, and a cool breeze played around us as I heard Nabeel sharing what he'd learnt with Arpita. 'The purpose of life is to be happy with whoever is in your train compartment. People will come, people will go. Some will teach you what to do. Others will teach you what bloody not to. Maybe we should love them all!'

He was right. Whoever comes by, for however short or long the period, invest your time to make them happy in the present. Don't waste your time trying to change the past. The past is the destination that has passed. Our life's train only moves forward. Once we understand that, we have everything we need to build a truly beautiful life.

• CHAPTER 7 •

The PARADOXICAL PRE-INTENTION FUNDA

ON THE OCCASION OF MY NINTH BIRTHDAY, WHEN I FIRST saw the spread on the table, I was pleasantly surprised. My friends from school, Asif and Javed, were coming home to celebrate the day with me. I'd expected my mother to prepare some of her delicious specialities, but had not expected my parents to bring out their finest ceramics and serving dishes for the occasion. Then I spotted something that sent me into a fit of rage.

In one angry swoop, I yanked the fine lace cloth off the dining table. The homemade lamb rogan josh, the heaped plates of kebabs and the biryani that had been lovingly layered in the bone china crockery hurtled to the floor. Along with the food, down went a bottle of sherbet, the vibrant arrangement of roses and gerberas, and my birthday cake.

My mother rushed in from the kitchen when she heard the crashing sounds of crockery breaking. She was aghast at the mess. Three hours of patient cooking lay scattered all over the floor, and pieces of broken glasses and crockery were strewn around. 'What's wrong with you?' she said angrily.

'Mummy, you don't care about my birthday. Look at the cake. See! See the size. What's the point in saving money by making a half-pound cake? I told you that I wanted a two-pound cake,' I howled.

My mother had a lot she could have said to me at that point, but she probably didn't want to ruin my birthday. She said calmly, handing me a thousand rupees, 'Bhai, it's your birthday, please don't be upset. I'll clear up the mess. Here, use this to treat your friends to a good dinner. Have a nice birthday.'

The next morning, she sat me down and asked me why I'd behaved like such a spoiled brat. I was feeling foolish, too, but explained that I had been embarrassed because the cake was so small. 'Mummy, what would my friends think of me? Of us? That we are poor and can't afford a big cake, even for special occasions.'

My mother laughed. 'My dear foolish son, if your friends minded the cake being small or you being poor, they wouldn't be friends with you, would they?'

I realised then that my mother hadn't intended to hurt me by baking a smaller cake. I was very sorry for my thoughtless and destructive behaviour.

It's easy to understand and rectify situations like this, because they are in our control. We can learn to rein in our anger and work on our character defects. But what do we do when someone is deliberately trying to harm us or mess with our minds?

During my college days, a disgruntled ex-girlfriend of mine grew resentful and started spreading rumours about me. She befriended a boy who didn't like me and garnered the support of his friends. Together, they indulged in a full-fledged character assassination campaign, with no holds barred.

Though I was initially taken aback, I was certain of some things I would and would not do:

1. Those people who believed the lies would not matter to me. I was fully aware that people see only what they want to see. The people who disliked me anyway would believe the rumour, without bothering to corroborate the truth. Any story, however flimsy,

would be good enough to convince them to accept the rumour as the gospel truth.
2. I would not speak negatively about the person who started these rumours. I felt that it would demean my relationship with my ex-girlfriend if I bad-mouthed her. Furthermore, I believed that negativity is not good for us, and that no person was worth being negative for. In any case, adding to the negativity would only add fuel to the fire. I'd rather let them gather their own firewood to keep their inferno blazing.
3. I would stay focused on my intentions. To graduate from medical college, take care of my family, devote my life to the recovery of drug addicts, and to be in a constant state of gratitude and love. Nothing was going to change that. Nothing.
4. I knew that in any situation, good or bad, people respond according to the expected magnitude of an event and not the probability of its occurrence. Therefore there would be no point in deliberating on reducing the probability of what may happen. I just went to the worst-case scenario in my mind—of what she could possibly say or do—and reduced its magnitude. *Que sera sera!*

I must admit that I was deeply hurt for a few days. Someone whom I had loved with all my heart was trying to destroy my reputation. It honestly didn't matter to me if they succeeded in their mission. I didn't really give a damn about what people thought or might start thinking about me. I just could not accept the fact that someone who was once so close to me was instigating others to hurt me.

Fortunately, my friend Vaaz, who knew about the rumours, shared a brilliant strategy with me. She called it the Paradoxical Pre-intention Fundamental Rule.

She explained, 'You can't stop anyone from messing with your head. Negative people are negative people and they love to put others down. It makes them feel good about themselves. The only thing you can do, when someone is trying to sully your name, is to give them permission (in your mind) to try to mess with your head.'

GIVE THEM PERMISSION TO TRY TO HURT YOU.

'Don't give them the permission to hurt you. Only give them permission to try. When we permit others to do anything, we feel we are in control. Then we can actually sit back and enjoy our sanctioned actions. After all, we have given them the permission to do so.'

I must admit that it was a mind-blowing strategy. By using Vaaz's paradoxical pre-intention fundamental rule, I actually started enjoying their moves. Seeing them try very hard to mar my reputation became a source of humour for me. Since my permission was restricted to them trying, I didn't get disturbed by what they were actually doing. At times, I genuinely felt bad for my detractors, as I knew they were simply misusing their time. The hours they spent on whisper campaigns could have been spent on so many of their other goals in life.

Unanswered questions pose serious complications and give birth to nervous energy. They always made me turbulent. I would wonder, 'I was so good to that person. He should actually be in a state of gratitude. Why is he acting like an ungrateful retard? Why?' My brain would go berserk trying to figure out the answers.

The questions would inflame a further battery of questions.

'What did I do wrong?'

'Why is this person being so mean?'

'What could have caused this sudden change of behaviour?'

The questions would never cease. The best tactic to calm the turmoil is to answer the question. It doesn't matter what the answer is. Perhaps someone is being mean because they are unhappy, or because they are fearful. The cause is unimportant—assigning a cause is key.

Our brains like certainty. Answer the question with any explanation you like. The brain will feel satisfied. The question, 'Why is he acting like an ungrateful bastard?' can be answered simply, 'Because he is an ungrateful bastard.'

No one can be certain of the reasons behind the actions of others. Sometimes, we do not understand the motives of our own actions.

I have developed another strategy now to add to the paradoxical pre-intention fundamental rule. It helps me deal with actions I don't understand.

I have created an imaginary folder in my head where I keep actions that I cannot comprehend. I simply recognize that this data belongs to the folder titled 'Things that will never be understood'.

I know that the act of this person can never be understood. Understanding that I will never be able to understand is also a kind of understanding.

This wisdom gives my brain a sense of control, and peace.

· CHAPTER 8 ·

EVEN the MOON HAS a DARK SIDE

XIMENIA GUADALUPE ALONSO WAS ONLY FIFTEEN WHEN her street art caught the attention of the residents of her hometown, Puebla. In the next decade, Puebla, the city of angels, famous for its cathedrals, Talavera pottery and Poblano sauce, had added another tourist attraction: the street art of Ximenia Guadalupe Alonso.

Her art travelled across the highlands of south-central Mexico and soon spilled over the Mexican borders. A number of European and American tourists visiting the country travelled to Puebla to experience the wall paintings.

Most of her paintings were anti-establishment. She was regarded as an activist–artist. Her parents were government officials, but she didn't enjoy the perks they were awarded by the Mexican government. She preferred travelling by public transport. Her social media posts were advocacy pieces through her medium of choice: art. She wrote about all forms of oppression.

The Organisation Mondiale pour la Paix (Organisation for World Peace) offered Ximenia a staggering 150,000 euros to create twenty-five artworks for them. The pieces would be installed at their headquarters in Paris. Ximenia accepted the offer. *El Universal*, the local daily newspaper, carried the story. The news spread like wildfire through Mexico.

On Twitter, she received a lot of negative reactions.

'Sad news! You belong to street art.'

'Don't ditch the movement.'

'The French are the enemy. Remember the war of 1862.'

She knew that she was doing the right thing in committing to the world peace assignment. Yet, these random tweets bothered her. Her state of mind was akin to the Puebla landscape: riddled with volcanoes as well as snow-capped peaks.

Her social media account had over a hundred thousand followers. She didn't even know who these people were. She had never met them. Yet, now she was bothered by their disapproval. She hadn't flinched at the anticipated backlash when she'd supported the 12,000-odd striking workers at the Volkswagen plant. She had not even bothered about the reactions of the Mexican government or the Sinaloa drug cartel to her street art denouncing their activities. What was the problem this time?

Why did these random tweets disturb Ximenia? There could be two reasons. One, her faulty relationship with money. Two, fragmented self-validation.

I can identify with both the reasons.

When I was growing up, my father would often tell me that one had to work hard to earn money. 'Good money doesn't come by easily. If your sweat falls to the ground while working, it is good money. Bhai, money doesn't grow on trees and is not carried by bees. You have to struggle to earn the money. Corrupt politicians, smugglers and drug traffickers make easy money.' For many years, I grossly undercharged for my services and struggled to make ends meet. This perfectly fit my father's description of 'good money'. Subconsciously, the absence of physical strain and exertion made me uncomfortable earning money from my patients. I had wonderfully rigged my circumstances to be in a state of constant monetary deprivation. It made me feel good. The struggle added meaning to my life.

In the early days of my career, many patients would ask

me, 'Doc, why do you charge so little?' My wife would also question me repeatedly: 'I do a simple government job; how come you make less money than me?' I had no answer. Only after years of conducting daily therapy sessions with my patients did I realise that I had a problem.

I had a block about money. Subconsciously I believed that 'money' was a bad thing to possess. Several patients of mine came from wealthy families and they were exceptionally good human beings. Experiencing them punctured a hole in my negative belief. One can earn 'good' money without sweating or manual labour. Any money earned without compromising on one's values is good money.

Ximenia was, deservedly, going to be paid for her expertise. Her activism saw light due to her ability to express her thoughts through art. The activism didn't drive the art. She wouldn't lose her ability to express her thoughts through painting if she was going to be paid for it. She wasn't committing a crime. She was following her passion.

Ximenia did have self-validation. Though, as in my case, it wasn't a hundred per cent. She could empathise with others easily. She was perfectly non-judgemental. With others. The problem was that she couldn't empathise with herself for the mistakes she'd made in the past. She continued to think of those 'Ximenia mistakes' as horrible acts.

There were two consequential ones that she hated the most. She had cheated on a boyfriend once during her teens. And her behaviour during her alcohol binges was antithetical to the general values she prided herself on. She had subsequently given up alcohol completely, and forgiven herself for her compromised actions. She was certain that the events wouldn't ever recur. But she didn't like the Ximenia who had committed those actions. She looked down upon that Ximenia.

But, when the social media comments began to disturb her, she realised that she had to first empathise with Ximenia of the past. She had to revisit those moments when she did those 'horrible' things. Get into her shoes at those points in time. Try to understand why she did those things, without justifying her actions.

She went back to the point in time when she had cheated on her boyfriend. She empathised with the girl who deceived her partner. Little Ximenia had poor self-control and a huge ego. She had been hurt by her partner's words the evening before.

She didn't justify the action, but merely saw little Ximenia's point of view. Then she started to accept and love that imperfect Ximenia. She stopped being severe with her.

Two things happened in an instant. The first was that she didn't reject little Ximenia. She loved her despite her flaws. The second outcome was that she saw how much she'd grown since those days, how far she'd travelled from being that egoistic girl to this genteel, kind and understanding human being. Then she empathised with herself for her alcoholism, and for every other thing that she'd done wrong. Over the next few days, she developed a hundred per cent self-approval. She didn't require any external validation for what she was going to be or how she lived her life.

'Even the moon has a dark side and I know that side is beautiful too,' she told herself.

Laying a white plastic sheet on the floor, she covered it with black paint. After the paint had dried, she used her thumbnail to carve out a curved line that revealed the white below. Digging her nails into the plastic, she began moving her hands like a maestro performing an orchestra for the earth beneath it. She scratched the black off the plastic sheet in smooth moves. The hours flowed by. Soon, a beautiful work of art was ready for installation. A phoenix, rising from the ashes.

Thank you past-me, you did the best you could have at the time. You've grown from your weaknesses to become this stronger-than-ever version of me.
For being you, thank you *

• CHAPTER 9 •

The Life Force, Within

THE ENERGY SOURCE THAT BREATHES LIFE INTO ALL OF US IS referred to as 'soul', or *rooh* or *atman* by different religions. Whatever you call this life force, it does exist. I have felt its absence every time I have encountered death. I felt its absence in my father's corpse and in the bodies of several other relatives, including my mother, my brother and my younger sister. The only difference between my father after his death and my father when he'd been alive was the absence of motion. He was not breathing. Rigor mortis, or the stiffening of muscles and joints, sets in a few hours after death, and that is when a dead body actually starts to look like a dead body, not earlier. It is evident that the only thing the dead body lacks is the animating energy.

All living beings have a material part (body) and a non-material part (life force or soul). The material part needs material nourishment while the non-material part needs spiritual succour. Our bodies require material foods to subsist—carbohydrates, proteins, fat, etc. Non-material things like love, kindness and gratitude cannot satisfy the needs of the material body, like hunger. Conversely, the non-matter part of the body can be satisfied by non-material things only.

On a daily basis, all human beings perform a set of actions for the upkeep of their bodies. To keep their bodies clean and healthy, they brush their teeth, have a bath, eat food, etc. But what about their non-material selves? Why do we

If i remember to keep nourishing this life force, connecting with and relishing its presence within me, i will always find my way back to it, to serenity ✳

assume that it does not require cleansing or nourishment? We keep adding material goods to our lives, to deal with our desires and fears. We feed our bodies and our egos, but why don't we cater to our souls?

An increase in material inputs, without simultaneous and corresponding inputs to the non-material self, only creates an imbalance in us. People who feel 'lost' have simply lost the balance between their material and non-material selves.

My idol, John Lennon, probably went through this polarity on a massive scale. At a very young age, he had obtained almost every tangible thing that a person could desire. He had everything money could buy and more. He had acquired all that appeals to a human ego: fame, recognition, and a superhuman status. Lennon and the other Beatles' members were showered with 'maniacal' popularity. They would be mobbed, felt up, jostled and scratched anywhere they were seen. Every teenage girl would have loved to take a piece of them home.

They mostly lived in hotels, recording studios and concert locations. They were so popular that there was a brisk trade in tiny inches of cloth squares cut off from the bedsheets upon which they had slept. The Whittier hotel bedsheets they slept on in Detroit is one instance of such ridiculous sales. Lennon was only twenty-four then. Even today, more than fifty years later, a square inch of the bedsheets the Beatles slept on is being sold as memorabilia for 950 dollars. I reckon that the more successful they got, the emptier they felt within.

Travelling to India for a spiritual search in 1968, Lennon soon found and lost—first Maharishi Mahesh Yogi and then drugs. Maharishi was easy to set aside, but giving up drugs required a long and sustained battle. It was during Lennon's fight with drugs and his subsequent recovery that he learnt to nourish his non-material self. He was forced to look within and nurture his soul.

For his recovery to be complete, he had to resolve his childhood conflicts and learn to be kind to himself. He had to grasp the concept of nourishing his soul by seeking non-material rewards. When he obtained spiritual growth, he was lost no more. The balance between his material and non-material self was set right.

Anything that offers non-material gains nurtures the soul. This includes meaningful relationships and being kind to family members, strangers, animals and even plants. Meditation and chanting. Prayer. Any positive action that doesn't generate a palpable reward feeds the soul.

Theosophists believe that the soul is connected to the body by an invisible chord attached at the umbilicus. This chord snaps at the time of one's death. The soul remains earthbound for a period of time after that. The length of this time, they deem, depends on how attached the person was to material things. If one was very attached, then the separation of the soul from the body is difficult, like a plum seed being removed from a raw plum. For a spiritual person, the soul moves out like a plum seed from a ripe fruit. Those souls that remain earthbound after dying are neither here nor there.

A hypothesis for the soul is based on the theory of matter and anti-matter. This theory postulates that since there is a universe of matter, there should exist a universe of anti-matter. If the two do exist, then there would be a high-energy bond between them. An infinitesimal part of that energy is what we call the soul. When we die, the energy returns to its source. If we assume that it takes about n number of seconds to return to its source, and if another human being is born in less than n seconds, the energy transfers to the person. This probably explains reincarnation. However, I do not subscribe to this theory.

Many other theories have been proposed to explain what

happens to the life force after death. I do not know which of them is correct. It doesn't really matter, as none of the variables scare me. Everything in our universe follows the laws of cause and effect. Matter and energy are both subject to the laws of the universe.

But one thing is for certain. When we die, our souls will not be confined to the physical space of our bodies and will be freed. And our current actions will never be divorced from our souls. The way we live our lives will guide the soul's journey into the unknown. An unknown of boundless beauty and peace.

We have come from this wonderful unknown. There surely has to be a good reason for it, for us to give up our freedom and be confined to a body. Birth cannot be attributed to chance. We all have our own reasons to be born.

I have found mine. I have found peace.

• CHAPTER 10 •

SHRINK THE RASCAL

A PATIENT OF MINE—LET'S CALL HER OLIVIA—CAME TO ME with troubles that are, tragically, all too common. The day we met, Olivia was trembling with emotion, so much so that a streak of sweat rolled down her right temple.

'Bastard! He is a horrible person. I can never ever forgive him. The lecherous swine was secretly screwing my best friend over the last few months of our relationship. I can't forgive him. The swine! I was just a trophy for him to show off to his friends. He didn't love me. He's ruined my life. Just give me some medicines to make me feel all right. I cannot deal with this anymore. Please prescribe something very powerful. It should just knock me out.'

The betrayal occurred over two years ago. Since then, Olivia had done everything she could to forget the episode. I could feel her pain, and told her what I had learned first-hand.

'Medicines won't help. You have to learn to deal with your issues. If someone doesn't understand mathematics, what pills can I prescribe? The only solution is for that person to learn math. Pills can help you forget that you do not know math—but pills can't teach you math. You have to learn how to deal with your issues. There is no point in taking a pill to forget that you have unresolved problems.'

Olivia had spent a year visiting multiple psychiatrists. They gave her varied combinations of anti-depressants, mood stabilisers and anti-anxiety pills. The medicines made her drowsy and she would zone out. But the drugs couldn't address the core question.

She wanted to erase all memories of her boyfriend Mikhail. The harder she tried to forget him, the harder it became to do so.

Olivia was clearly an emblematic case of experiential avoidance. The more one tries to avoid an experience, the more powerful it becomes.

'In order to move on, Olivia, you will have to forgive him,' I said.

'No way. I have to let him off the hook after what he's done to me? I have to accept that he was right?' Olivia was incredulous.

'Quite the contrary. You have to accept that he has wronged you and let it go. Forgiving someone doesn't mean that they are right. It means accepting that they are wrong, but letting bygones be bygones. If you aren't able to do that, you will constantly carry him and his actions in your mind. Aren't you pegged down by audio-visuals of the harm done to you, running in never-ending loops? Olivia, these negative loops fuel more negative thoughts, which then cascade into unbearable negative emotions. Isn't that what's happening to you?'

Olivia was silent and I continued: 'As you want to obliterate the "Mikhail experience", you keep trying to distract yourself from thoughts that are related to him. It works for a while, but then they promptly return. You've created a rule in your mind: 'Don't think about Mikhail'. To follow the rule, you have to refer to the rule.

'Your rule is such that you have to keep referring to Mikhail. You feel perpetually trapped. Trying to avoid thoughts of Mikhail hasn't worked for you so far. Medicines haven't worked for you either. Right? Why don't you try a different approach?'

She turned to me. 'But how? I would if I could, but how is it possible to forgive Mikhail? Even the smallest thought of him makes my blood boil. I can feel palpitations coming on when you say his name.'

'If you pardon him, you will be a higher soul, won't you?'

Olivia was puzzled. 'How do I become a higher soul?'

I walked around to her side of the table, and raised my hand above her head. 'If I were to forgive you, it would be like this. My hand would be above your head. I'd have to stand at a position higher than you. I wouldn't go on my knees to forgive you, would I?' I said, dropping onto my knees on cue.

Olivia chuckled. 'That's funny, Doc.'

'It's funny, but it's also true! You have to assume an elevated position to forgive someone. You become the stronger human being. The person you are forgiving is weaker than you.'

To understand the root cause of Olivia's problem, we must understand how the human brain stores memories. The moment we are born, our brains start recording data. Our eyes function like video cameras. Whenever they are open, they record everything in their line of vision. Every frame the eyes record is downloaded into the memory data base within our brain. This recording makes up zillions of video bytes per day.

Our ears function as audio recorders that are always on, even while we are asleep. An additional zillion bits of audio bytes (data) per day are being continually streamed into our memory data base. Tactile, gustatory and olfactory data also add their data bits, as and when they are perceived by the brain.

These gazillion bits of data that are being recorded also have to be easily retrievable. The only way our brain can do it is by storing them intelligently—to use an analogy, in files of various sizes. It devotes more space to important data, and this is saved in bigger files. These files that are important (charged with emotions) may be required at short notice (1/10,000th of a second) for survival. Assume that the most important memories are saved in folders according to the emotions experienced: fear, helplessness, hurt, anger, frustration, pain, and so on.

The folders have two principal sections. Memories with strong emotional content are stored as audio–video files. The episode of Mikhail's betrayal and other painful experiences can be recalled in three dimensions, in motion, and in colour. The files that do not have strong emotional content are stored in other folders. These memories are saved in smaller zipped files only as still pictures. They can be recalled as two-dimensional, black-and-white static pictures. These pictures are also graded by their importance. The least important ones are saved in very small sizes.

Top priority is given to emotional files that are tagged 'high risk'. These files contain 'threat' patterns that necessitate immediate responses. In Olivia's case, 'betrayal', 'rejection', 'snake', 'gun', 'murder', 'palpitations' and 'Mikhail' would be some of the files that were tagged 'high risk'. All of them would elicit the same response. Whether Olivia was in the presence of a snake, or merely imagined that a snake was nearby, or had a thought about Mikhail, her body would react in the same way. The flight response triggered by her sympathetic nervous system would increase her blood pressure, heart and respiratory rates, and the blood supply to her limbs. An avalanche of neurotransmitters would reach all the cells in her body within a few seconds.

Whenever new data is registered by the brain, it first finds a matching pattern and then stores it as a file in a folder that contains similar matching patterns. By doing so, the brain recklessly opens files with similar data (situations

If i try not to think about them, i end up constantly thinking about them. i am now choosing to confront and shrink the demons of my past. i am choosing to forgive and let go ✱

and responses) from the past that are stored in that folder. Then the brain reacts to the combined threat responses saved in the folder. But Olivia would not be conscious of all the data she was responding to.

Olivia's rule, 'Do not think about Mikhail', became a filter to look for patterns similar to anything connected to Mikhail.

- Faces like Mikhail
- Body language similar to Mikhail's
- Mikhail and sunset
- Mikhail and brown hair
- Mikhail's likes
- Mikhail's dislikes

Countless combinations of Mikhail patterns fit the rule. Unknowingly, she kept thinking of him all the time. As long as Mikhail was perceived as 'high risk', her brain would keep looking for him in people, places or things in an attempt to protect her from the potential menace. The key to Olivia's release from her pain was to stop perceiving 'Mikhail and his related data' as a threat. This was possible if all the 'Mikhail data' was transferred into files in the unimportant folders of the brain.

There was a simple technique that Olivia could employ.

1. Closing her eyes, she could revisit the betrayal in her mind. She would see the scene as a three-dimensional colour film. Perhaps she would see Mikhail and her friend hugging each other.
2. She could stop at any one moment and freeze the frame. She could then visualise just a photograph of them hugging.
3. She could then focus and remove the colour from the photograph and 'see' the black-and-white picture for a few seconds.

4. The next step would be to slowly shrink the photograph. That life-size picture of Mikhail could be downsized by a foot. Staring at this smaller Mikhail for a few seconds, she could now continue to gradually diminish his size further. Repeating the procedure over and over, Mikhail's size would eventually be about an inch above the ground—and in black-and-white.
5. The last step would be completed after she looked at the tiny picture for a few seconds and then imagined that she could see it vanish.

If she repeated the procedure a few times, the brain would recognise the tiny black-and-white pattern and would transfer the data bits, according to their size, to another storage section. As only unimportant folders are stored in this section, she would respond accordingly. She would be able to remember the negative event, but it would be devoid of any emotion.

As there was no threat or negative emotional content, the brain would soon regard Mikhail as a non-threat. So instead of avoiding thoughts of Mikhail, Olivia should allow them to surface and follow this procedure. Each time, she should shrink the rascal into a one-inch black-and-white figure in a photograph, before making it disappear. Within a few days, her mental agony would be over. The rascal would become extinct.

• CHAPTER 11 •

The Spirit of Creation

OVER TWO THOUSAND YEARS AGO IN GREECE, SOME OF OUR ancestors prayed to Priapus when they were unable to conceive a child. A large percentage of those women who believed and performed the arduous rituals got pregnant soon after. Priapus was the mighty god of fertility. Ancient murals depict the god with an enlarged penis: Priapus has a constant erection.

How did the women get pregnant? We can safely rule out one variable. It's unlikely that the god of fertility paid an inconspicuous visit to the family home and had sex with them. Incidentally, the enlarged and constantly rigid penis might be indicative of a penile disorder called phimosis. Anyone with that condition is definitely going to be infertile, as he would suffer a lot and would not be able to endure the pain of copulation.

So how did the rituals work? Why did it not work for some? Was there a common denominator linking the failures? What was the secret? Was there a right and a wrong way to do the ritual?

My deduction is that it worked for all those who believed that it would work. It is their belief in the deity and the rituals that worked. The magic was in their own beliefs, not in the power of the deity.

A majority of the heroin addicts I've treated over the last thirty-four years have not experienced any 'turkeys' or withdrawal symptoms when they begin the detoxification programme. I am certain that it is not the combination of medicines that I administer. Why? Because when some addicts relapse and try to detoxify themselves elsewhere, with the same medication that is prescribed at our rehabilitation centre, they go through severe withdrawals. Even those who take twice the prescribed dosage go through the same unpleasant physical and mental reactions.

If it is not the medicine working the magic, then what is at work? It's the same thing that works for the Priapus believers. It's not me. It is their belief in me. Most of my patients have been referred by other recovering addicts who have not experienced withdrawals. They, too, believe that they will not go through withdrawal. Therefore they don't.

I am not implying that people get whatever they want. They do not. They get whatever they believe they will get. Belief is everything.

Genghis Khan's belief that he could conquer millions of square kilometres of territory and create a mammoth empire is the reason why he succeeded. In the process, the Mongol emperor unleashed ruthless wars reported to have resulted in the deaths of more than forty million people.

Genghis Khan's belief-driven conquests can be understood through the theory 'belief is everything', but what about the forty million people who were killed in those wars? Did they want to die? No. They did not want to die. They simply believed that they did not stand a chance against The Khan and assumed that they would be killed.

The power of belief is value-neutral—what you believe, whether life-affirming or life-threatening, is what you get.

Imagine the following scenario from the thirteenth century. For the inhabitants of Ein Qiniya, a small town on the Golan Heights in Syria, the day begins normally. David, a young shepherd, strolls lazily up the knoll chewing dried Esfand seeds, thinking about the upcoming annual cattle auction.

His thoughts are interrupted when he sees a cloud of

dust in the distance. He can hear what the village chief had told them, the fearful tales passed on by Al-Adnan, a trader of spices who traversed the Silk Road. A new merciless military power from a faraway land was advancing towards Eurasia. The Mongols were known to annihilate everyone who stood in their path, Al-Adnan had told their chief.

David stands paralysed, unable to count the thousands of warriors on sturdy horses galloping up the rising path. The scorching sun glints off their lances. The white light refracts through the dust rising from the hooves of the thundering steeds and, for a moment, David fears that a ghost army is marching up the slopes. Could he be hallucinating? The Esfand seeds had induced him to see visions before, but they were never so potent.

David gapes at the invaders, disbelief holding him frozen. Adrenaline pumps into his bloodstream as thoughts of the foretold massacre floods his consciousness.

The Mongols raise their giant catapults on the far range. A cadaver thuds down upon the ground, just a few hand's breadth away from David, jolting him out of his stupor. Scurrying down the slope he howls, 'The Mon...Mongols are comingggg!'

At his cry, the settlement plunges into chaos. People run helter-skelter. Some collapse where they are standing, shrieking and wailing in terror; some stand frozen as the shock to their nervous systems hold them immobile. A few rush out with daggers and swords.

It takes the army less than a quarter of an hour to unleash a rampage of horror. All the town's inhabitants are slaughtered. The Mongol warriors annihilate all life, and vanish in the direction of Abu Qashsh, a city two miles to the north.

The massacred Syrians had believed that they could do nothing. They had no doubt that if they ever encountered the Mongols, they would be killed.

Only Maalik and his graceful wife Laneke are unharmed in the attack. When Maalik was nine years old, he had stumbled upon a secret, hidden cavern, just a short distance from their town. He firmly believed that no harm could come to him in that space. It was his safe haven.

When Maalik sees a panicked David scampering down the slope, it prompts him to act immediately. An eagle-fletched arrow whistles past his right shoulder. He seizes Laneke's arm and yells: 'Run!' As the siege rages on behind them, the couple races to Maalik's 'safe haven'. He firmly believes that they would be secure there. They were.

Belief is everything.

However, our beliefs are also subject to constant change. Our beliefs are fluid and influenced by the nature and sources of data inputs to our brain.

I think that for the past two decades, I've been in a good state of mind, barring a few blips.

The streams of data could be love-based (+ve) or hate-based (-ve). A majority of the data is fear-based. It induces passivity and further magnifies all negative emotions like fright, panic, jealousy, despair, helplessness, anxiety, anger and hopelessness, to enumerate just a few. The negative data stored in our brains from the past, originating from our beliefs and experiences, is further strengthened by the data coming in through the world.

Parents are the chief sources of data for preschool children, who later get influenced by their schools, peers and friends. The media controls and dominates most of the data for the rest of our lives.

Like our genes, our memes (systems of behaviours) are also passed on from generation to generation. Today, mass media thrives on fear-based data for eyeballs and profits. Unknowingly they contribute to the insecurities of populations agglutinated to them.

Since the function of our brain is to protect our body,

it relates more easily to threatening data, by eliciting flight or fight responses. This creates a colossal vicious cycle that produces more negative responses. These escalate from individuals to populations almost instantaneously, as in the case of Genghis Khan's victims.

How does one sustain positive beliefs with the negative inputs that keep erupting from multiple sources on a daily basis?

I attribute my positive beliefs and their sustenance to all my life experiences. Hundreds of people, numerous books, and scores of hours of listening to music.

The positive state requires constant, proactive inputs, and mindfulness.

The teachings of J. Krishnamurti and my interactions with drug addicts in recovery were some of the initiators. Krishnamurti's concept of getting rid of psychological time and being in a state of *observing* made it easier for me to become less reactive.

In the earlier years of our drug prevention campaign, lots of time and energy were wasted in trying to get the enforcement agencies and the government to act, and to engage the media to write about the perils of addiction. Deliberations on the role of the government, corrupt politicians, media and even mafia dons were routine. But these deliberations didn't change much on the ground. I felt more fulfilled when I was working directly with addicts and their families. The recovery of one addict would create a ripple effect that touched the lives of hundreds of other people connected to her and her family.

My inferences from Krishnamurti's teachings helped me find a solution to this mindfuck. I substituted 'responsibility' with 'response-ability', or the ability to respond to any situation, no matter who was responsible for it. I fully understood and accepted what I could do and what I couldn't. Since then I have devoted my life to the cause

As i draw from life to learn from it, i also now draw my reality into being with the brush of my thoughts. i'm beginning to imagine better for myself, and what i believe becomes. i'm creating consciously, mindfully, steadily, lovingly *

of drug prevention and run a modest rehabilitation centre, reaching out to thirty addicts at a time. I focus on the lives of people that I can reach out to, which doesn't even constitute a small fraction of the total number.

Yet, I feel at peace. Every single life that turns around is very significant in my reality.

Our prevention campaigns cannot quantify the number of school and college children who will not experiment with drugs. It's easy to count the number of schoolchildren who become drug users but not easy to calculate the number who will turn away from drugs, never use them, and spare themselves years of waste and struggle. No one will ever notice the gainers. No one has to.

The philosophy I've imbibed and experienced over and over again is that it's good to be good for fuck's sake. In fact, if we are good so that people are good in return, it's manipulation.

I have also learned to be positive from people whom I've met only through books and music, and texts I've read. They make an exhaustive list. Below are the pre-eminent ones.

Rudolf Clausius and the second law of thermodynamics, which taught me that all states in our universe are going from less entropy to more entropy.

INFERENCE: The universe is constantly changing its state—from less chaos to more chaos.

Albert Einstein's theory of relativity and his thought experiment with Nathan Rosen and Boris Podolsky which explains 'the entanglement of quantum particles'.

INFERENCE: Everything is relative and everything affects everything else.

John Lennon's lyrics:

Life is what happens to you while you are busy making other plans.

– and –

Love is the answer.

INFERENCE: Self-explanatory.

Mohandas Gandhi's non-violent movement and its contribution to India's independence.

INFERENCE: Don't feed wood to your enemies' fires. Don't fight negativity with negativity.

The Mahabharata.

INFERENCE: If our five senses (Pandavas) are controlled by our intellect (Krishna), we can overcome any struggle.

A lot of deliberate action is required to warrant continual positivity. Some of the measures employed are discussed in separate chapters of this book.
- Meditation
- Prayer
- Being in a state of gratitude
- Being real

When I was much younger, I thought that life was like a football match. There are two teams who play for a win. The good guys and the bad guys. We get to become part of the good guy team and win the match. For the first four decades I devoted myself to this philosophy and did everything I could to make sure that the team of good guys won.

Ignoramus that I was in the spiritual plane, it took me over forty years to figure out that there were no teams. That I did not control anything. That I cannot control anything. No matter how my senses perceive control.

Perhaps I'm just the football field where the match is being played, and everyone and everything is entangled in a perpetual cosmic dance.

Everyone has their own set of swings and turns that are an important part of this shimmer. Through the dance, anyone can prize whatever they want. *All they have to do is believe.*

CHAPTER 12

FREQUENCIES ARE RETURNED TO THEIR POINT of ORIGIN

ANDRE WAS LIKE A YOUNGER BROTHER TO ME. I LOVED him, but he was irresponsible, indisciplined and lethargic. He was studying to be a Physics major, but was debarred from his examinations because of his dismal attendance record. His antics were a constant source of misery for his parents, who were as close to me as my own mother and father. The idea of a job didn't appeal to him. He thought there were more meaningful things in life for him to do, like road-trips and drinking with his friends.

He believed that his parents were duty-bound to provide for all his needs. They were not supposed to 'interfere' in his life by asking him any questions. How, where or when he spent their money or his time was none of their concern. He loved his 'sponsored independence'.

Andre died because of his alcoholism later in life. But, before that, before his actions became habits, I wish I had known what I know now. In the years ahead, I would meet patients who would be able to change their lives when they discovered a different way of looking at the world.

Sometimes the catalyst for change is as small as a conversation, which leads to an action taken, and a different set of choices being made. Just as a one-degree change of course is enough to send a ship to a new destination, a small change can go a long way. This is how I imagine Andre's life might have gone differently.

AN IMAGINED CONVERSATION WITH MY DEAD 'KID BROTHER'

'You simply love the chaos in your life,' I say.

My words anger him. 'You think I'm crazy to like chaos. You think I love this mess. You think anyone likes chaos?'

'Andre, if you don't love chaos, why are you attracting so much of it into your reality? We attract everything into our reality. Our sorrows, our joys, people, things...everything.'

'That's bullshit,' he says. But there is doubt in his voice.

'If you give me a patient hearing, perhaps I will be able to convince you of the truth. If you promise to listen intently, there is a chance that you will realise how powerful you really are. You will be able to achieve whatever you want.'

Andre likes that bit about being powerful. He drops his usual bored pose. 'So how can I attract everything I desire? Tell me, Bhai, how long will it take me to get what I want?'

'How long will it take? Or how powerful can you be? What should be the question? Do you mean to say that if it's going to take some time, you don't want to attract good things into your life?' I ask.

Andre is disconcerted by my sharpness.

'No, I didn't mean that. I'm all ears, take your time. For the first time in my life I'm getting a good vibe, like something enormously good is going to happen to me,' he says. He mimes a happy dance, still sitting down.

'VIBES. VIBES!' I yell, startling him. 'Do you know what can happen if you vibrate your fingers 20 to 100,000 times per second?'

Andre stops gyrating his hips. He thinks about it. 'If I move my fingers 20 times per second, it would appear to be a blur.' Then he laughs: 'But at the speed you suggest, I suppose my finger is going to fly off my hand!'

I laugh with him. 'Just imagine if it is possible, Andre. Assume there is a machine that can move an object that fast. You know, the vibration will turn into sound. The sound would be audible to us humans if the vibration is in the range of 20 to 20,000 times per second. The higher vibrations would still be sound but audible only to dogs and bats. Bats can hear higher frequencies, ultrasonic vibrations till about 100,000 times per second.'

Andre is interested despite himself. 'Wow! That's pretty cool stuff. This kind of justifies your doctorate. I like this vibration and cosmos shit. So what happens next?'

Gratified by these signs of attention, I warm up to my subject. 'You know what happens if you escalate the vibrations drastically? If you can speed up the vibrations to 430 THz (trillion times per second), it would not be sound any more—the vibration would transform into red light. Taking it higher up to about 550 THz modifies the vibrations into green light.'

Andre wraps his mind around these concepts, tripping on what we're talking about.

'Everything in the universe is a vibration. It's easy for our minds to accept that gases and liquids are in states of vibration. But both states in a confined space would require electron microscopes to actually confirm that they are in motion. Solids, too, are also constantly vibrating. All matter contains electrons that are constantly changing their positions.

'Thought is also a vibration. An EEG machine (electroencephalogram) that is used to detect epilepsy also confirms that there is electrical activity in the brain during thought.

'When we switch off a light bulb, it goes dark. However, the emitted light vibrations from the bulb continue to travel into the universe at 186,282 miles per second. They will do so forever.'

He interrupts me. 'Wait. You mean to say that when the light in a bulb goes off, it is still going out into the universe. Why can't we see it?'

I explain that the light he sees radiating from the stars are actually coming from the past. Some of the stars we see today don't even exist. They died out millions of years ago. We are merely seeing the state they were in once upon a time.

'Really?' Andre says. Then he frowns. 'This is cool, but what's the connection between this stuff and vibes?'

'Well, just like light vibrations, every time we think a thought or feel an emotion, we send its vibration out into the universe forever.'

'I believe that this leads us to an even more interesting chain of thought:

'That the vibrations of positive thoughts and emotions are higher than those of negative ones.

'That when we are in a state of negativity, we feel and emit low vibes into the universe.

'That we can even sense not only our own vibrations but also the vibrations (vibes) from the people we encounter in our daily lives.'

Andre interrupts: 'Yes, I know what you're talking about. I have experienced vibes. You know when I am enjoying myself, and randomly feel a negative vibe? Sometimes, I feel the vibe of a person's presence just before the person actually comes within my range of vision.'

'Me too. Our thoughts and our emotions emit specific vibrations or frequencies. These aren't restricted to our surroundings—these reverberations travel throughout the fabric of the universe. We are constantly tuning the frequency of our FM broadcasts into this time–space continuum.

'We can only receive our specific frequency from the plethora of frequencies in our universe. When we emit positive vibes or vibrations, we are setting up a positive vibrational frequency. Then we can only receive positive vibrations back and vice versa.

'A person from Los Angeles who dials someone in Shanghai will only reach that single number in Shanghai through the maze of over seven billion frequencies. Today, there are more mobile phones than people in our world, but no other mobile will catch the call.'

I turn to him. 'How do you process this data? What sense does it make to you?'

Andre is juiced by the question. He stares at the ceiling, trying to find the best words to express his thoughts. 'The universe is connected to me through my vibe. When I think an angry thought or feel angry, the universe responds by creating a situation that justifies the anger within me. So if I'm angry, the universe creates more situations that make me angrier.'

'And what happens when you are in a state of gratitude?'

'G...r...r...attitude! When we are in gratitude, we send out a different frequency. It's like changing your mobile number.'

'The frequency of gratitude will only receive signals of gratitude.'

'Hey, that means the universe will create situations that will simulate our gratitude! Bhai, does it mean that we can fool the universe with our thoughts and emotions? We can just think or feel gratitude and the universe will create situations for which we will be grateful?'

I say, 'That's possible.' We spend some more time together, chatting about other things before calling it a night.

Later, Andre is hard at work, writing down the highlights from our chat so that he doesn't forget. This is what he wants to remember:

Emotions are more powerful than thoughts in creating realities, as emotions are E + Motion, energy in motion.

One should try to be grateful as often as one can.

One should proactively smash negative thoughts and create positive thoughts.

One is attracting events into one's life simply by thoughts and feelings.

He closes his diary, placing it on the bedside table. As he prepares to sleep, a strange thought comes to Andre. Good vibes—who knew that you could get them from stuff other than booze? He feels better than he's felt in months of partying, energised and curious. Man, he thinks, you can get good vibes through good thoughts and good conversation! What a trip.

Shuffling through his music collection, he selects a beloved track, Led Zeppelin's *'Stairway to Heaven'*, and presses play.

...and he's buying a stairway to heaven.

༄

CHAPTER 13

Learnings from an Orange Tree

I CORDIALLY INVITE ALL READERS TO PARTICIPATE IN A thought experiment. For this experiment, imagine that you have been given one million orange seeds.

Imagine that you have unlimited resources and unrestricted access to the entire database on our planet. All the support you need will be provided. The seeds can be planted at any place you choose. You can plant them on the earth or on any habitable planet in any of the multiple universes.

Assume that you have managed to plant the entire lot. It's probable that not all of them would have germinated. In fact, not all of the saplings that have germinated will grow into trees. Of the ones that do become trees, not all the orange trees will bear fruit.

The probability of an orange-bearing tree would depend on a multitude of factors: the potency of the soil, the availability of water, the weather conditions, etc.

The trees would probably grow to varying heights. Though a majority would stand in the range of 18-22 feet, the number and length of branches in the different trees wouldn't be exactly the same.

But what is the probability of just one of the million seeds evolving into an oak or a banyan tree? Or any tree other than an orange tree? Zero per cent. That possibility does not even exist.

The laws of the universe are the same in the physical and the mental dimensions. In the physical universe, when we sow orange seeds, we don't reap bananas or elephants. In the mental universe, if we plant good deeds we only harvest good deeds.

Let's assume the point in time an orange seed is planted is referred to as the impact point. The laws of the universe ensure that it will turn into an orange tree, but the tree isn't going to spring out of the ground at the impact point. It may take over a year to attain a height of one foot and an additional four or five years to bear fruit.

Although it's guaranteed that the seed will grow into a tree, it will not happen instantaneously.

The planter can howl at the sapling, threaten it, or sing hymns glorifying oranges. ('Oh mighty orange, thou art the fruit of life', etc.) Even doing a rain dance around the tree won't make any difference. Nature will dictate its course.

Even doing all of the above religiously, for days on end, will not alter the fate that nature has predetermined. Nature has no consideration for the patience threshold, the religiosity, or the intelligence quotient of the planter.

When you sow the seeds of hard work, its evolved form will materialise into a tree bearing fruits of success, but not at its impact point, as in the case of the orange tree or any other creative process.

Remember my patient Olivia whose boyfriend cheated on her? Olivia was wedded to the 'what you sow is what you reap' philosophy. Her philosophy worked wonderfully well, until the fateful day when she experienced a betrayal. The hurt of the betrayal amplified her pain. 'I must be doing something wrong. I must've planted pain to reap so much of it,' she thought.

Her mind space was occupied with thoughts of her black swan. Its retrograde predictability further intensified her suffering. She refused to let go of her 'what you sow is what you reap' philosophy. What had she sowed to deserve this horrible harvest? She spent futile hours scanning her mental database. She believed that she had done nothing so terribly wrong to be inflicted with so much pain. She also strongly believed in the laws of cause and effect. Her mind was on overdrive.

What was the missing link that connected her two diametrically opposite and conflicting beliefs?

She focused hard and scanned her brain memory.

'If I was sitting under a coconut tree and some coconuts fell on my head causing it to bleed, I wouldn't think it was because I must've lacerated someone's head in the past. The coconuts that fell on my head wouldn't be considered as agents of revenge in nature's tit for tat.'

What was she missing? A flash of Jesus crucified on the cross came to her mind. According to the orange-seed theory, what did Jesus do that was so wrong that he was betrayed by Judas and then subjected to the torture of crucifixion?

What we sow is what we reap. Jesus surely couldn't have sowed such seeds of bad actions that evolved into the tree of torture in the final stages of his life. That simply wasn't possible.

Olivia examined the event at the impact point. There were no answers to justify the suffering of Jesus. When she decided to step away from the impact point and then see the crucifixion, she understood the law of reciprocity. She was delighted as she now saw the event's consequence hundreds of years later. The seeds of torture had evolved into a beautiful tree—a religion called Christianity. Jesus wanted to spread Christianity; the crucifixion catalysed his desire.

She knew then that the pain of being betrayed was good for her, but she was feeling miserable. She realised that at impact point it was impossible to understand how or why her betrayal was a good thing. But what if she tried to see these events far away from the impact point? Then they would appear to be very different. She guessed that this period of vulnerability might contribute to her becoming a better human being. 'Perhaps I'm being sensitised for the good things to come,' Olivia thought.

In order to cope with her pain, she attended meditation classes and prayed regularly. Proactively she encouraged only positive thoughts. Six months later, she experienced herself as an evolved person. Fuller and happier.

Today, she thinks that the betrayal was the best thing that ever happened to her.

CHAPTER 14

Jaikishan & the Ant

IF YOU MET JAIKISHAN KAPOOR TODAY, YOU'D NEVER believe his story. He runs one of the most popular restaurant chains in Europe, and he has the look of someone who enjoys eating the gorgeous food his home-style restaurants serve. His patrons queue up on Friday nights for his pasta specials—and for his impromptu jam sessions with the bass guitarist. Joltin' Jai has a voice like Little Richard, a belly laugh all his own, and a love for old rock n' roll that his audience laps up.

When he takes to the dance floor, he makes everything shake, rattle and roll. I've seen him charm imperious Italian contessas into doing something called 'the frug', but then he could charm a swarm of bees into giving him their last drop of honey. 'When Joltin' Jai laughs in Rome, they can hear him in Budapest,' one of his hundreds of admirers told me once.

He's the last man you'd imagine would attempt suicide, and yet, there was that one time when he almost took himself out of the game. But let me tell you the story the way he narrated it to me.

'I was taking a flight from New Delhi to Rome,' Jai said. 'Imagine that! One of the world's most romantic cities—and all I could think about as they announced boarding for flight EK 513 was my suicide plans.' He laughs.

It was almost midnight, and his staff were closing down Ardente. Giovanni brought us two macchiatos and some biscotti and, as a final touch, flipped a Louis Armstrong record on the jukebox. We often stayed on long after the restaurant closed for the night, chatting about life, the universe and everything, but this was the first time Jai had shared his past in such detail.

'I was travelling first class,' he said. 'That would have excited me in my twenties, but that day, I barely noticed the comfort, the luxury, the discreet service. I had thought about nothing but my suicide all week, and I'd planned it carefully.'

He had bought high-dose sedatives at various chemists, and transferred the capsules to a bottle of digestive medicine. 'The first thing I did once we were in the air was to take the bottle out of my bag. It brought me comfort to hold it, knowing that the pills were there as I repeatedly rehearsed the suicide. I didn't switch on that fancy TV set; I couldn't tell you today who my co-passengers in first class were.'

It isn't easy to imagine Joltin' Jai, large as life and twice as handsome, in this state of mind, but he sketches me a picture. He was listless, perhaps his hands were clasped tightly together, maybe the corners of his mouth twitched ever so slightly. I imagine that he was consumed by self-pity and negative thoughts about himself.

As if he's heard my speculations, Jai said, 'Now I can't believe how repetitive and whiny my thoughts were! All through the flight I was thinking:

'Nobody cares for me.

'There is nothing that is mine.

'I don't deserve to live.

'How could I be such a bastard.

'Nobody understands me.

'Living is unbearable.

'Why am I so abnormal?

'I mess up all the time.'

He laughed, shaking his head in disbelief. 'Hell, I even whispered to the capsules: "You guys can help me make her suffer." That's what I was thinking—*Aditi is going to regret this.*'

'That was on your mind all through the flight?' I asked.

He nodded. 'That, and other negative junk. At one point, I went to the bathroom. I was walking like an old guy, you know. I remember staring at myself in the mirror, full of anger. Not at Aditi—at me, myself.

'I still remember what I said to my reflection: "Bastard, you deserve to die. You have done nothing right in your life. You are a horrible human being. No. You are not even a human being; you are an animal. You possessive and cruel son of a bitch, you deserve to die. Thank God your wife left you. No one loves you."

'See, no one interrupts you in the first-class bathroom. You can sit there as long as you want, and it's private. So I could go on and on at myself: *It's her fault, too. She didn't understand my insecurities. I love her. She doesn't even know that. She has to know that. She must know that she is responsible for my death.*'

Jai took a sip of his macchiato and tested the crumb of the biscotti against his broad thumb. 'Then, guess what? I took my wedding ring off, dropped it in the toilet and pulled the flush! I went back to my seat and typed out a suicide note on my iPhone. It was quite something. I'd got to the part where I wrote, "Please do not do a post-mortem of my body to ascertain the cause of my death. To find the real cause of my death, do a thorough examination of this letter. My wife Aditi…" when the air hostess tapped me gently on my shoulder, asking if I'd like something to eat. I said no, and switched off my phone. I didn't want her bothering me, so I pretended to sleep. When I woke up, the pilot was making the announcement to land. So I finished that damn suicide note in the Emirates business class lounge, in the smoking section.'

'You used to smoke, Jai?' I asked.

'Not anymore,' he replied. 'Terrible habit, I want to live a long and happy life!' He laughed at the irony of it. In that Dubai lounge, he'd given no thought of the life that lay ahead of him.

Instead, he'd finished typing his note. He'd closed his eyes, reciting it from memory. 'My wife Aditi is responsible for my death. She could have given me one more chance. What's the use of feeling guilty when I'm no more? I know she is cringing now, as she is watching my dead body and pictures. She has to live through Black Diwalis now. Honey, now you know that I died in Rome, the city of our honeymoon. The city that was a witness to the promises that you have broken.

'I did everything that we had done on our first visit. I even checked into the same hotel. Now you'll be crying forever. You will never be able to forgive yourself for my death.

'Papa and Ma, I didn't have a choice. I apologise for this death and for all the times I've troubled you. I really loved you. Trust me, I wouldn't have killed myself. The pain of a life without Aditi would have been unbearable.

'I really loved you, Ma. I know that you will take care of Papa. Forgive me, if you can.

'Aditi, I know I will burn in hell now. But you will burn on earth for the rest of your life too. God will never forgive you. Aditi, if you had given me a chance to change, all this wouldn't have happened. My rage was just a reflection of my emotional wounds. You wanted me out of your life. I have done as you had wished. Now I am no more. Goodbye, forever.—Your dead husband, Jai.'

'It was so full of drama,' he said now. 'And I missed

all the fun of the flight from Dubai to Rome! It was my first-ever flight in an Airbus A-380. That's such a luxury, but all I did was recline my seat to a 180 degree, lie down, and rehearse my suicide all the way. It was quite a plan. I was going to retrace every single thing we'd done on our honeymoon. Then I'd buy a knife, go to the hotel room, and take the sedatives. Immediately after taking the pills, I planned to send that email with the pictures of my Rome Honeymoon Rerun Route to Aditi, copying all her friends. I had it all worked out—I was going to turn off my mobile, slash my wrists for insurance in case the pills weren't enough, and the rest would be up to Yama. The point of it all was to make Aditi suffer.'

'And that was all I could think about. The plane landed in Rome—I was envisioning how Aditi would feel when she saw the pictures of my dead body. I was sure the police would show her every last gory one.'

'It didn't work out that way, thankfully,' I said.

'Life can surprise you,' Jai said softly. 'It sure can.'

He'd booked a room at Hotel Fontana. In the lift, he felt the memories flooding back. It was a small lift, just four feet by four feet. 'We were on our honeymoon, that first time we were at the Fontana,' he said to me. 'There were our two big suitcases in that tight space, and the two of us squashed together. Sometimes it's the small things women do that you remember forever. She'd given me the most sheepish smile, apologetic, all the way till the lift—it was old and slow—halted on the second floor. It had been the most magical beginning for us.'

I watched my friend's eyes soften. 'This was seven years later, seven years after our honeymoon,' he said. 'I had suicide on my mind, but when I opened the door to that hotel room, I swear it felt as though she was right there, holding my hand. I went in and the first thing I did was to open those tall windows and look out at the Trevi Fountain. She'd loved that. I felt the cold air flow in, and remembered how, all those years ago, I'd given her a small postage stamp with the image of the Trevi Fountain on it. She'd smiled at me, enchanted, curious.'

All through that day in Rome, I tortured myself, thinking of Aditi and me, and how we'd been. It started there in the room—remembering how I'd touched her cheek lightly with one finger, and she'd turned and surprised me by kissing me. We'd held each other in front of the Trevi; now standing there again, my thoughts were so bitter. I thought, she'll regret everything, she could have prevented this so easily.'

He did carry out a part of his plan. He stopped at the steps of the Trevi Fountain, recalling how Aditi had tossed a coin over her left shoulder, promising that they would be together 'till death do us part'. Local legend said that if you made your wish before the coin fell into the pond, you'd come back to Rome with your wish fulfilled. 'She'll come back to Rome for sure,' he thought with bitterness, 'after death has parted us.' He took a photograph of the fountain, and walked to the pizzeria, barely twenty steps away.

Aditi had loved the way the server used giant scissors to cut the pizza into rectangular shapes and then weighed each slice on a scale. They had asked for two portions of Potato Pizza. They had kissed on the bar stools in the corner. They'd been madly in love.

He'd ordered some pizza, sat on the same bar stool, and taken another photo, thinking, 'Soon she'll see this, soon she'll be crying.' Then he'd dumped the pizza in the garbage bin on his way out.

'I spent the next hour walking around the city until finally I sat down on the freezing marble floor of the Piazza Novona. Aditi had exclaimed over the sculptures, and I'd taken over a hundred photographs of her and the fountain, delighted by her delight. I was crying quietly to myself, wondering why she had to kill me, why it had to end like this, when I remembered the knife. I'd forgotten to buy the knife!'

'I rushed off to Cucina near the Spanish Steps—Aditi had bought crockery from there. I chose a ceramic knife, imagining how distressed she'd be when she saw how I'd used it. She would be crushed, I decided, and the thought made me smile.'

Jai looked out over the squares, so old, so beautiful. The tourists had gone, but there were still some locals hanging around, telling each other stories. We heard a loud roar of shared laughter, and it made the place warmer, happier.

'You believe in coincidences?' he asked, then he answered his own question. 'Maybe we get more chances than we realise in this life. See, I'd decided I would slash my wrists at 8.30 p.m., because we'd got married at that exact time. I had an hour till my deadline, so I sat down on the Spanish Steps to wait until it was time. I could see the church at the top, and I had harsh thoughts for God. "Even you can't help me, God!" I said to Him. "You, too, betrayed me. You have all the power to change her mind, but you didn't do that." I thought no one was watching me so I cried, a little, quietly. I had the sedatives in my overcoat, the knife in the Cucina bag by my side.'

He looked back at me, and smiled. 'That's when it happened.'

'"Jai? Jai!" the unexpected sound of my own name rose clearly across the Steps. Startled, I looked around. There was a group of Chinese tourists, taking photographs, a bunch of friendly, laughing teenagers, two locals perched several steps above me.

'"Over here, Jai! Look here, you fool!" I saw this Chinese guy frantically waving his hands above his head—

unbelievable, but there he was. Zihao, my former roomie from Boston, running down the stairs. "Zee!" I yelled, and then we were hugging, laughing. Before I could say much, Zee was marching me away from the Steps.

'"Jai, this is too good to be true. You have to meet my wife and son. My son was a little under the weather, so they're resting at our hotel. The Ambasscotri, you know it? So where is Mrs Jai? Shopping?" he smiled.

'I took a quick peek at the time—6.45 p.m.—and then I found myself telling Zee the truth. I always told Zee the truth, back in Boston. "Actually, my divorce decree came through the day before yesterday." Zee just looked at me. "Shit happens, man. Tell me about it." He sat back down on the step and waited. Zee was always easy to talk to, so I didn't hold anything back.

'"I'm feeling lost, Zee. I'm a loser. I fucked up. She left me. There is nothing that is mine. I know I was very selfish. She didn't want me," I said.

'Zihao leaned backwards, "Man, you got such a big ego."

'"What? I got a big ego? She has a big ego, not me. I apologised to her, countless times. I was ready to do anything! She refused to get back with me," I said. My voice was shaking.

'But Zihao touched my arm lightly, and though his voice was sympathetic, he didn't soften what he had to say. "Come on, Jai. All the sentences that you've uttered so far have either begun with 'I' or ended with 'me' or 'mine'. Am I correct?"

'I was going to respond angrily, but instead, I felt this rush of sadness. I couldn't hold my tears back. I sobbed on my friend's shoulder like a child.

'Zihao let me be for a while, and then he did the damnedest thing. This visualisation exercise! I didn't want to, but if you ever met Zee, you'd know that he's gentle but forceful. He wouldn't quit and finally I agreed.'

'What did he ask you to do?' I asked.

Jai said, 'I remember it so clearly. It was real simple, but hey, it worked. First, Zee said, "Close your eyes and imagine you are on a beach front. Can you see the waves?" So I did as he said, but it didn't work out too well.

'"I can see Aditi on the beach, walking away from me," I said, glumly.

'Zee was firm. "Screw Aditi, man. Please, Jai. The entire exercise won't take more than a minute. For friendship's sake, man."

'So I closed my eyes and tried to imagine the beach. "I can see the waterfront," I said hesitantly.

'"That's great!" Zee said. "Imagine a table floating in the water."

'That seemed really strange to me, but I obediently closed my eyes again and soon I could practically see the table floating on the ocean. I gave it rough timbered legs, and a sleek black polished top. "Now imagine an ant on the table," Zee suggested. This was much easier.

'"Focus on the ant. Look at the ant moving across the table. Notice it trying to avoid the splashing water. Can you see it? Good. Now, imagine that the table is floating away from you. Focus on the ant as the table is receding slowly into the distance. Now imagine that the table is so far away that it is as small as the original ant. Just a small speck in the ocean. Yes?"

'Zee waited for a confirmation from me.

'My eyes were squeezed shut. "Yes, the table is now a tiny dot."

'"Open your eyes," Zee said. "When the table was the size of a dot, how insignificant was the ant on it?"

'I thought about it. "The ant was almost non-existent."

'Zihao laughed. "Buddy, at that point in time the ant was considerably more significant than your presence on earth. *Drop the ego, man. The ego is the root of all pain.*" I must have looked perplexed.

"'Come on man, let's go. My wife and son will be wondering where I am." It was when we'd both got up that I realised my shopping bag was missing. Zihao shrugged it off: "The probability of having your pocket picked in Rome is greater than the probability of having a pizza in Rome!" I wasn't amused.

"'Did you lose something precious?" Zihao asked.

"'Yes. It was my ticket out of this life. I had bought a knife to kill myself," I said. I looked at my watch. It was 7.15 p.m.

"'Oh," said Zihao as we walked towards his hotel. "But it wouldn't work for you because you're a good human being."

'I stared at Zee, confused. First ants, then this "good human being" business. "What? I don't get the connection!"

'Zihao said, earnestly, "But you have to be a horrible human being to successfully commit suicide. The effect of suicide in the afterlife is dreadful. Your soul stays earthbound and repeats the last five minutes of your life over and over again until the time for your natural death is reached. More than painful, I guess it would be eternally boring. Jai, even if you had a terrible illness and tried to end your misery, you would first be subjected to this tedious loop and you would be born again with some disease. The cycle of cause and effect has to be completed, my friend.

"'There is no escape. There are no exceptions. Think clearly, you are not going to end your suffering, you are actually going to prolong it. Muslims and Christians believe that it is an unpardonable sin that guarantees you burn in hell forever. You don't want that, right? Is proving a point to your wife worth all this shit?"

'I wanted to protest, but somewhere deep inside, I wondered, what if he was right? If there was even the slightest chance that some of what he said was true, I didn't want to take that risk, frankly.

'Zihao said, "Buddy, if you're doing this because you want to ruin your wife's life, get real. She will probably cry for a few days and carry on with her life. The human brain is tuned to look away from disasters. It's your parents who will suffer. I am sure you do not plan to repay them like this. Back in Boston, you'd told me the trouble they had gone through to afford your education at Harvard."'

Jai turned to me. 'All that time, I hadn't thought about this? I'd been imagining the effect that my death would have on my wife—but I hadn't given a thought to how it would impact my parents. That shook me. But I had one last doubt. That's what we humans are like, there's always some little thought lurking at the back of our minds!

'I asked Zihao, "But tell me one thing: when the photos of my dead body flash across TV channels over and over again, won't that haunt my wife forever?'

'Zihao thought that was the funniest thing ever. "Who the fuck do you think you are, Jai? The president of the United States? Some international rock star? CNN, BBC and all your Indian channels are not interested in suicides committed by nobodies like us. That's hardly news. Even Trump's obnoxious statements have a three-day value. Why do you think he keeps on making stupid and ludicrous statements? Come on, it's time for dinner."'

Joltin' Jai smiled at me. 'That's how it ended. Zihao was a good friend, and he was also smart. We stopped on the way so he could tell his wife he was going out with me, and we had a great, simple meal: pasta in one of those classic Italian sauces. Then he tricked me into eating even more with an ice cream challenge. We had eight rounds of gelato, and it was much later that I realised what he was doing.'

I said, 'Is your friend Zihao a doctor?'

> PLEASE LEAVE YOUR SHOES* AND EGO OUTSIDE BEFORE YOU ENTER

* BECAUSE HOW WILL YOU STEP INTO ANYONE ELSE'S SHOES, IF YOU'RE WEARING YOUR OWN?

i'm only a tiny speck on the magical shimmer of this vast multi-faceted multiverse. Realising that i is not the centre of it liberates me — to be an observer, to just enjoy the myriad shades of its expression *

Jai said, 'Yeah! How did you guess?'

I said, 'Because with the ice cream and the extra sugar, he'd decreased the blood supply to your hyperactive brain. Your stomach must have been distended, which would increase the blood supply to the abdomen.'

'That's correct,' said Jai. 'Zee said his grandfather, his Zufu, often told him, "Whenever you're stressed, you must eat lots of ice cream." It was 11 p.m. by the time we finished. I went back to my hotel, after promising to meet Zee and his family the next morning at 10 a.m. There was one last thing I had to do before I went to sleep. I stopped by that beautiful fountain, fished the bottle of sedatives out of my overcoat, turned my back to it and tossed the bottle over my left shoulder. Of course, I made a wish. I figured if it worked with coins, it would work with sleeping pills.'

He locked up his big restaurant, and we walked towards his home, a large, beautifully decorated apartment. Even at this late hour, he was greeted with warmth and affection by the few locals around—'*Buona notte*, Jai!' they called out merrily.

'I guess it worked,' he said to me. 'Smell that perfumed night air. Remember that Louis Armstrong song we were listening to? It's true—it's a wonderful life.'

∾

III. INSTANT KARMA

getting there

• CHAPTER 15 •

CERVANTES & the UGLY DUCKLING

'YOU CAN NEVER STRAIGHTEN A DOG'S TAIL, EVEN IF YOU place it in a pipe for six months. When you remove the pipe, the tail will still be curved. Your ears are made of flexible cartilage, stupid. They will stick out again. Remove those ties and go to sleep,' said my elder brother, Suleman.

I had wrapped two of my father's ties tightly around my forehead, trapping my ears in between them. My large ears were sticking out even more thanks to the sudden appearance of oval bald patches on my head. I was losing hair in chunks. I was only ten. I hated what I saw in the mirror.

The pain I felt was intensified by my schoolmates' reactions. Some children can be very cruel. They would flick my ears from the back and laugh. I was conscious of my ugliness and people around me made me feel like the Elephant Man, Joseph Merrick. They would stare at me in wonder. Heads turned when I walked past in the school corridors and canteens, on the streets, and in public buses. Wherever I went, I felt people around me laughing as they enjoyed the freak show. I detested looking at anyone; I stared at the feet of every person I met, not wanting to meet their incredulous gazes, or see the pity and disgust in their eyes. My self-esteem had plummeted well below zero.

I was in intense emotional pain. My mind was in its vice-like grip whenever I left my house. I didn't know then that the same area of the brain, the anterior cingulate cortex, lights up when one faces physical pain or when one goes through the pain of rejection.

But, in reality, I was no 'Elephant Man'—but perhaps more like the ugly duckling in Hans Christian Andersen's fairy tale. All I had to do was to find my own kind. And in order to do that, I had to start looking at people around me. I couldn't afford to look away any more. I had to find my kind.

Even though it hurt to meet their eyes, I started noticing the other boys in the public bus to school. And soon I spotted a boy who was fully bald seated two rows ahead of me. He seemed happy. Frantically, I looked around—how were others in the bus reacting to the boy? No one was staring at him!

Bingo. My patches were creating the freak show. As I'd started losing hair, I had turned very possessive of the hair that remained. It was the haphazard display of those bald spots interspersed with patches of hair that looked so odd. I decided to go bald. Showtime was over.

The only problem now were the large ears. There had to be someone whose ears stuck out as much as mine. It took me two months of research to realise that I was in august company. I read somewhere that Miguel de Cervantes, who had authored the classic novel, *Don Quixote*, had large ears. So did Prince Charles. Wow! I didn't feel like such an ugly duckling any more. Perhaps I was a beautiful swan. A bald one, though.

Medications and injections were flown in from the UK. Vitamin supplements, light therapies and even vigorous massages were suggested and followed. Not a single hair follicle appeared. I believed that the hair would come back. I knew I was destined to greatness like Cervantes. For that, I had to have a pleasing personality—I couldn't be scary, like the bald Yul Brynner as Rameses II in Cecil B. DeMille's *The Ten Commandments*.

I was ready to do anything to get my hair back. An Ayurvedic doctor suggested to my father, 'Get some *jamalghota* (croton tiglium) seeds. Put some drops of lime on a hard surface and rub the seeds on it to form a paste. The pulp should have the consistency of toothpaste. Apply just a coin-sized patch on the scalp. He is likely to get high fever, but do not give him any medicine. His scalp will burn. The next morning, his fever will go, a rash will erupt and within a fortnight, hair will appear through the rash follicles. Follow the same procedure until he has a full head of hair. Keep a gap of two days between applications.'

My father laughed after the doctor left. 'Bhai, I know about these jamalghota seeds. We give it to our horses for treatment of constipation. It's a powerful laxative. The guy is nuts.'

'Please, Baba, I want to do the procedure,' I pleaded. We had tried so many things before that. 'What's the worst-case scenario? It won't work. Please Baba, I feel terrible.'

The following day, we followed the instructions to the letter. The fever came and went; it was followed by the rash. Then the hair! Within two months I had a richer harvest than I had ever sported before. Six months later, I had a good crop of hair, ears like an accomplished novelist and a prince, and the self-esteem of Andersen's ugly duckling at the end of the fairy tale. I was ready to spread my wings and fly.

There was a fallout of the experience, though. I had been over-sensitised to pain and rejection. I knew how people suffered when they were hurt. So I felt the need to be nice to people, and I became a people pleaser. Over a period of time, this need created more pain than the hurt I'd felt during the 'Elephant Man' phase. My niceness made people take me for granted. That upset me tremendously. I would go out of my way to do things for others. This stayed with me for a long, long time.

I would parry compliments. I felt very uncomfortable when people thanked me for doing something good. I'd go out of my way to make people believe that they were helping me when I was helping them.

My father could not send me to MIT (Massachusetts Institute of Technology) because we didn't have the funds. I'd felt miserable then. Many years later, I sent three students to study abroad. All of them are still convinced that I have been able to relive my life as a student due to their generosity. As the song goes, 'I like it like that!' They are free to ascribe any reason to my decision to have funded their studies. It does not matter.

But often, by trying so hard to be nice, I created a few bums and monsters. By overpaying a staff member and overlooking his misdeeds because he was poor, I eventually brought out the monster in him. People you are excessively nice to, at times, begin to resent your niceness and, strange as it may seem, some of them even start assuming that they are being controlled by you. They stop taking responsibility for their own actions.

After many lapses, I finally got sick of this staff member's non-compliance and fired him. He applied for a position elsewhere, and wasn't able to procure even one-fourth of the salary I'd paid him. Unable to accept that he'd been drawing a higher salary than was suitable for his abilities, he felt great resentment. This staff member is still certain that I was the one who ruined his life. Mark my words, whosoever you are excessively nice to in this fashion will eventually resent you.

In the past, I always thought that being nice was a good thing. It isn't. Being decent is. What's the difference between the two? Being nice to someone only makes the other party feel pleasant. You have to be agreeable and accepting all the time.

Being decent involves three factors:
1. Being kind
2. Being civil and polite at all times, and
3. Being just and fair to both parties concerned

When one is nice to others, one is not fair or just to oneself. That's where my problem was, and it's a problem shared by many. Many drug addicts and alcoholics I encountered were like me: they were 'nice' people, they were hurt people. Soon I realised that I had more in common with addicts than with Mahatma Gandhi, Barrack Obama, Daniel Craig or Will Smith. I certainly had ears like the Mahatma or Mr Obama, and shared their sense of commitment, but in many other aspects, I was closer to addicts. I belonged to the flock of addictive personalities. I shared their extreme behaviours, their sense of rejection and abandonment. I, too, was once enveloped in that muck of pain.

Over time I've perfected the art of brushing off the muck. I share the learnings with my flock, as a part of my life. We understand each other very well. We are the ugly ducklings. We are the beautiful creatures.

For all my kind out there: You are not alone. You never were.

∽

CHAPTER 16

My Mother's Secret Marriage

I SAW MY FIRST BLACK SWAN BEFORE MY THIRTEENTH birthday. I discovered that my mother was secretly married to another man. The finding sliced me into multiple insecure wedges haphazardly strung together by guilt and shame. It decimated my faith in human relationships. In God. In everything.

Over the next two decades, I had a couple more of what I think of as black swan events, in the shape of unnerving betrayals. In a lifetime of meeting and befriending hundreds of people, there have only been a very few of these unexpected, unpleasant experiences where people I had reason to trust could not live up to the faith I had placed in them. Today, I thank God for all of them. Why? Simply because these events have helped me evolve into the human being that I am. I love myself immensely. I can share so much more with the world. This wouldn't have happened if I had not had these apparently negative experiences.

I now know that I was not an exception. I was not the only person on this planet who felt betrayed. Almost all human beings experience a few betrayals in their lifetime. Even prophets have had their share of betrayals: Jesus had his Judas.

It is our response to these powerful adverse events that determines whether we sail or drown. They are milestones in our lives, points in time that mark a cardinal change in our thought patterns and the course of our lives. These are gifts from the universe that help us evolve.

My mother's betrayal took me more than a decade to assimilate. Other subsequent experiences were relatively minor in comparison and were resolved much more quickly. Initially my response was to shut out the event from my own consciousness. I would try to remove my focus from the negative experience, keep myself as busy as I could, and immerse myself in my books. Basically pretend that it didn't matter at all. However, these evasion strategies actually added to the misery.

Looking back, I can see that with all these events, their retrograde predictability further magnified my pain.

When I was a young boy, my mother would leave our home every night and come back the next day. I found this daily disappearing act quite odd. I asked her why she had to go. She said that all mothers leave at night, to stay in their fathers' homes. I believed her explanation, even though it didn't make sense. Deep inside, I knew that something was amiss. When I discovered the truth, every one of those memories came flooding back, stinging me with the pain of rejection.

I don't know why I felt ashamed of my mother's secret marriage. It became my secret too, a stifling secret. Everyday life became laborious. I felt that nobody should ever know that my mom had cheated on my dad and us siblings, by getting married to another man. The only way to keep the secret was to keep my 'friends' off my home turf. In order to achieve this, I had to spin a continuous web of lies. By my teenage years, I had created a false image of myself as a cool dude who loved adventure, fun and deviance, the kind of person who hated to be at home with his old-fashioned parents.

I projected my parents as monsters, who fought constantly

and created violent scenes at home. I repeated the lies so often that soon I started believing in them. That made me even more miserable.

No one knew the real story, the real me, or what I really felt. My fake self had many 'friends', the real me had none. I felt lonely, unloved and outcast.

I don't know how or when I perfected the art of mismanaging relationships, especially with the opposite sex. The secret of 'being cheated on' weighed heavily on me. I had developed serious trust issues. The aim of all of my early relationships with women was not to create love or togetherness; it was 'not to be cheated'.

This had classic consequences. I would invariably only be attracted to girls who could potentially cheat on me. If they didn't, I'd behave in a manner that would make them leave me. Then I'd feel cheated. Everything had to work out in accordance with the script I was reliving over and over. I only realised this in retrospect, after I had reappraised the incident of my mother's cheating on us. This was a decade and a few betrayals later. After her demise.

I had to be honest with myself if I wanted to stop living in misery. It couldn't be just bad luck that all my relationships followed almost the same pattern. They began as a perfect ten. Soon, I would sense some behaviour in them that reminded me of my mother's selfishness. Then I would start feeling insecure which would result in outlandish behaviour. The women would get fed up of my tantrums and decide to leave. I would feel cheated. I would always feel as helpless and angry as I had when I'd discovered my mother's second marriage. The finale was always the same: it would end with me blaming my mother for my misery.

I had to give my relationship with my mother far more solemn thought. It wasn't possible that betrayal was all I'd received from my mother in all these years. I wasn't

Superboy, I certainly hadn't taken care of all my needs from the day of my birth. I couldn't have possibly washed my ass when I didn't know where it was in the first place. Somebody must've done that for me, someone must have taught me how to walk, speak, read. I still don't know how to cook though!

When I examined my memory, it didn't take me long to start remembering countless instances of my mother's love and affection. I had blocked out all the loving times simply because I wanted to be angry with her. My brain had filtered those out and created a screen memory that screamed: 'As soon as I was born, she cheated me.' How crazy can we humans be when we want to give ourselves a reason to hold on to anger?

My thinking was incredibly distorted, and I allowed my rage to twist everything. When my mother had realised my plight, in the days when I'd left home and was living on the streets, she visited me in my medical hostel. She wanted to help, she wanted to give me fifty thousand rupees—a very substantial sum at the time. But I was so attached to the story I'd created of her betrayal that I refused to accept the money. To rationalise my refusal, I decided that my mother was trying to manipulate me. The money would make me complacent and take the sting out of my fight. Besides, I was going to make it on my own anyway. 'She wanted to take away from my self-made-man story. What a bitch!'

I still don't know how I made myself believe that shit.

Looking back, I see the endless number of times when she tried to make amends, actions that I had dismissed as 'manoeuvres'. Now I see my mother more clearly. She'd been there every morning when I woke up. She'd been there every afternoon when I came back from school. She only left at night, after putting us to bed. Wow! What a beautiful mother she was in reality.

If i can look my pain in the eye, really see its purpose and let go of the story i've been telling myself about my life, it loses its toxic hold on me. Then, from this moment on i am free to write a bright new script ✳

My parents were no longer alive, so they couldn't confirm what had really happened between them. But when I put together the facts in my possession, I had a reasonable hypothesis.

For reasons best known to them, they had divorced. She must have fallen in love again with another man. My parents must have decided not to tell their children about her second marriage until we were old enough to understand. They hadn't realised that my brothers and I would be curious, that we would play Sherlock Holmes and Watson; that wasn't part of their script. It must have taken great love on both my father's and mother's part to attempt to keep up this fictional story. They had done it because they wanted us to believe that we were a normal family.

The real issue was that a part of me had refused to accept the fact that my mother belonged to another family also. Finally, so many years later, I accepted this. It didn't feel good. I cried and cried. At first, I went through a barrage of painful emotions. I wanted to apologise to my mother, but I couldn't. She was no more. Then I thought of how the event had sensitised me to pain and loneliness. These intense emotional shifts in my understanding happened when I was in the early stages of my rehab career. This and a few similar events have only helped me to empathise better. They have turned me into a caring human being.

I learnt that the most powerful thing in the universe is love. Love is what I thought I had lacked throughout my childhood. It was always there, but my anger had blinded me from seeing it. Nevertheless, I understood the power of love in its absence. I started giving love to my patients. That's the magic potion: love is what works!

Another black swan event was when my dad threw me out of his house. After reappraising it, I realised that it was one of the most beautiful things that had ever happened to me. It motivated me to become the person I am, someone who tries every day to be a good human being. If it hadn't happened, I would probably have been an unhappy and ungrateful businessman today. The quality of my life would have been probably appalling compared to the serenity and contentment I have now.

I stopped taking things for granted and living life as a victim because I couldn't afford to do so any more. I had to survive. I had no other viable option but to complete my education in medical college.

The pain and the rejections that I'd faced were necessary for me to learn how to keep my head above water. The crises fortified my goal. The sharks in my tank made me a far better swimmer.

When I looked more carefully at the occasions when I'd experienced betrayal by people close to me, I could see how often I'd set myself up, ignoring the warning signs. I'd been faithful to that old, worn-out script, taking select events and tweaking them through my actions until they fit into the script.

Acceptance was the key that allowed me to open the doors and let the misery out. Change began to happen when I revisted all of this through a conscious process by which I looked at events in my life and assumed that they must have been for the best, since my present reality was working well. Taking a second look at life events was the best tool to exorcise the demons of the past that were torturing my present and that might have caused trouble in the future.

Today, hundreds of my patients have benefitted from these findings. Thank God these events happened to me. If I were to be born again, I'd pray for the same number of black swans—preferably, in the same sequence. A dozen more could be added randomly to boost the challenge. Amen!

• CHAPTER 17 •

The FLAVOUR of LOVE

'DAD, YOU OWE IT TO ME; I DIDN'T EVEN WANT TO BE BORN.'

'Aren't all parents supposed to look after their children's needs?'

'What's the big deal if you make sacrifices for my benefit? Don't all parents do as much?'

'After all, it's my right, as your son.'

'Whatever you give my brother, you have to give me the same as well.'

Ungrateful thoughts like these routinely occupied my mind till my dad threw me out of his home. Up until then, I suffered from a great sense of 'entitlement'. I took everything my dad did for me for granted.

He was supposed to do everything for me. I had nothing to be grateful for. In my view, he was dispensing his duties as a father. I was merely receiving privileges that were due to me. It angered me when he refused to comply with my demands. It infuriated me when he lost huge amounts of cash betting on race horses. I thought he was squandering 'my' inheritance.

My sense of entitlement probably crumbled the very instant the doors of my father's house shut on me. The resentment that I carried with me to the streets was slowing down my journey, draining my mental energies, and decreasing the odds of my survival. I don't know if I really discarded them eventually, or was side-tracked by my need to survive. I wanted to survive. I knew that I was going to.

Within the next six months I graduated from living on the streets to being a parasite in a hostel at my medical college. I shuffled through many hosts.

Human beings have a default negative setting. The brain looks out for threats to help us survive. I can't explain how, why or when my default negative setting changed to a positive one—to gratitude.

I began to feel genuinely grateful to my hosts, who let me sleep on a mattress in their rooms. I felt grateful to the students who paid me in food for the tuitions they received from me. I did not grudge the fact that they bought the cheapest item on the menu—*medhu vada*, a bright orange, crispy, savoury doughnut. That was my staple breakfast and lunch, and it was served with lots of free sambar, a filling curry of lentils and vegetables. I now realise why I had bright orange shit all those years! Three cheers for medhu vada–sambar.

For dinner, I prowled around alcohol parties at the hostel, eating the peanuts and wafers on display, while pretending to have a drink with my fellow students. Three or four good parties and dinner was done. I was grateful even to some of the guys who mocked me for being a freeloader, but didn't stop me from eating their nuts. I still don't know why people have to snack on fatty, salt-laden stuff when they drink alcohol, but I'm very glad and thankful that they do.

I was intuitively grateful all the time. This was not a strategy; I had simply fallen into a perpetual state of gratitude.

It was many years later, after I'd been working with addicts, that this time of my life would come back to me in flashback mode. There was a pattern of behaviour among substance abusers and emotionally dependent patients that separated those who recovered from those who relapsed. What made the difference was gratitude.

On the day of his farewell, the formal send-off we give patients who've graduated successfully from the rehab programme, Danny, a long-term heroin abuser, shared this with his batch mates: 'For the first two months or so, I was just whiling away my time at the rehab,' he said. 'I cursed the place, I was a pain to the others here, and I would circumvent the routine and share my negative world view with a few people who were in a similar state of mind.

'One afternoon, on my way to the gym, I noticed a small anthill. I stopped to inspect it, and saw hundreds of tiny ants filing out of the ground, following imaginary lines. Then a thought struck me. I should've been under the ground. Fifteen years of mainlining heroin and I was still above the ground. Alive, kicking, and cursing. I felt a jolt of intense gratitude. That's what kick-started my recovery. Everything seemed different. I was grateful to be alive and my perception of the world and everybody in it changed.'

Danny has been sober, productive and happy for over twelve years. He's never lost his sense of gratitude.

Danny was just one among more than a hundred recuperating addicts whose recoveries were fuelled by the awesome and positive power of gratitude. In retrospect, I realised that my default setting was the same. It was my decision to be always grateful that kept me charged.

Gratitude helped me stay focused in a positive zone. I didn't need to dodge the negative monstrosities that must have cropped up while I was setting up Land and learning to handle my patients and their families. I didn't even notice them. No matter how severe or distressful a particular event might have been, I only looked for positive outcomes. Perhaps that is why I saw only the good in everything that happened. Gratitude ensured that my attention didn't waver from my core intentions. It helped me keep my focus on the positive outcomes I intended in various aspects of my life.

I spent a lot of time and effort inventing ways to make my patients understand the power of gratitude and practise it on a daily basis. I consciously decided to help them inculcate gratitude as a strategy to combat stress and negativity in general.

Creating and constantly updating their sense of gratitude worked wonders for those who were committed to it. What was the logic? In order to remain in a state of gratitude, they had to look at life through a positive filter. There couldn't be any negative distraction that might swing them away from their goals. They were constantly looking out for reasons to be grateful. *Since we see only what we expect to see, they saw the good in everything.*

Imagine a hillside covered with only roses. No thorns, barbs, spines or bristles. Just love, positivity and bliss. Following the path marked gratitude. When you reach gratitude country, you would know what the real flavour is like.

· CHAPTER 18 ·

THY WILL BE DONE

I COULDN'T BELIEVE MY EYES. I HAD NEVER SEEN ANYTHING so scary before. The scene was reminiscent of Ridley Scott's 1979 horror science-fiction film, *Alien*. It seemed like there was an alien trapped in the patient's abdomen, wriggling, poking. Why was it moving about so frantically? To find a weak link to rupture and emerge out of his body?

The hemispherical lump was protruding about an inch from his abdomen. It changed its position rapidly. First it would trace a zig-zag pattern in the region that contained his small intestine. The bulge would appear at one place, and quickly move a few feet horizontally before vanishing. Then it would pop up in another part of the abdomen. Every few seconds, the bulge would reappear and disappear. What the hell was going on?

The patient was on Cot No. 3, tied down with strips of bandage. The stench of his urine mixed with the sharp smell of antiseptics punctured by his painful cries made me nauseous. I was frightened.

It was my third month as a resident psychiatrist at the psychiatric ward of the Sir J.J. Group of Hospitals. I didn't know what to do—but, thankfully, the senior nurse did. She calmly injected him with a shot of pethidine (a synthetic opioid analgesic). The lump disappeared, and so did the pain and the chaos. Soon, the patient slumped back, fast asleep. This heroin withdrawal was markedly different from the other ones that I had observed before.

Actually, all the withdrawals or 'cold turkeys' were dissimilar anyway. I read everything I could find on the subject, and finally learnt about the first heroin addicts on our planet. They were American GIs in Vietnam.

To garner the support of Burmese tribes, the CIA helped them to cultivate opium crops. They then taught them to convert the opium into heroin. In search of a readymade market to sell their narcotic produce, they sought out American troops in Vietnam. The first batch of heroin-addicted soldiers returning to the US reported mild flu-like symptoms. Body ache, a runny nose, mild fever, a bit of restlessness, and diarrhoea. It is reported that the government started a quota of heroin for these addicted soldiers. The withdrawal symptoms became more and more intense for subsequent batches of returning soldiers.

I soon realised that even the heroin addicts in India who came to me for treatment displayed distinct patterns. In addition to the documented withdrawal symptoms reported by American GIs, the chief complaint of patients varied according to the regions they came from. Addicts from Delhi complained of 'a large weight on the chest', which made it difficult for them to breathe. For the addicts from Bangalore, it was 'jelly in the legs' that hurt. For the addicts from Mumbai, the chief complaint was 'aching joints and severe abdominal cramps'. For those aware of John Lennon's *Cold Turkey*—'Temperature's rising/Fever is high/Can't see no future/Can't see no sky/My feet are so heavy/So is my head/I wish I was a baby/I wish I was dead…/My body is aching/Goose-pimple bone/Can't see no body/Leave me alone/My eyes are wide open/Can't get to sleep/One thing I'm sure of/I'm in at the deep freeze'—everything that the lyrics mentioned happened to them. Every single symptom.

I detoxified patients who were admitted to the psychiatry ward and also some who were outpatients. After participating in the detoxification of over two thousand heroin addicts, I came to these three conclusions.

1. Those heroin addicts who were physically restricted during the detoxification experienced massive 'cold turkeys'.
2. The trigger for the escalation of the cold turkeys was the patient's level of anxiety.
3. The belief of the addicts dictated the nature and severity of the withdrawal symptoms.

Another astonishing fact was that during their addiction, the addicts' 'cold turkeys' almost disappeared from the instant they scored the drug. No 'chasing' heroin. No injecting heroin. Once they had the substance in their hands, the 'cold turkeys' vanished. I guessed that this was because gaining access to the drug wiped out their anxiety. Or, was the hero of this strange story really their belief? Could the power of belief be that strong?

I started focusing on reducing their anxiety during the pre-detox phase. I invested time and effort in gaining the patient's trust. Till the patient trusted me and viewed me as a friend, I didn't prescribe any medication. I would advise them to use their daily quota (of the drug of their choice) but see me regularly. I would repeat these lines like a mantra: 'Don't worry about the cold turkey; make sure that you remain drug free. I'll knock the turkeys out with my medication.'

Within the first few weeks, some of the patients who came to me experienced only light withdrawals. This news spread like a virus within the community of addicts in south Mumbai. I soon learnt that addicts in Mumbai and a few other cities in India had christened me 'The God of Detox'. There was no visible halo around my head. Not even the faintest beam of light shining out of any of my orifices. I was no God. But they believed it to be true. Their belief worked for them.

By now, I had detoxified over 4500 heroin addicts. Whoever came to me for a detox didn't experience withdrawal symptoms. What could be the reason? The addict who didn't experience cold turkeys also didn't recover. Within a maximum period of a fortnight, he would return to his old ways. He went back to his regular hangouts and spoke about the painless detox he encountered to the addicts there. Hundreds of them all over the city and in other parts of the country were singing the same 'With Doc, No Turks' song. Receiving the same data from different people fortified their belief.

It was only when I realised that no addict could recover fully without a long-term rehabilitation programme that I stopped the outpatient detoxification programme. Dr Merchant's laundry service closed shop.

Belief was the critical factor that created the terrible withdrawal symptoms. It was belief again that lessened the severity of the dreaded 'cold turkeys'. Belief caused the excruciating withdrawals; belief caused them to disappear.

A decade later, as drug dependents and depressives started responding positively to our inpatient, familial behaviour modification programme, it had the same viral effect on the dependent populations. Our rehabilitation programme at the rehab that we lovingly refer to as 'Land' has an 85 per cent success rate today. Parents and patients believe that 'Doc works!'

I am Doc. I know that *I* do not work. It's their faith and belief in me and the rehabilitation facility that works. I merely share the thirty years of data that I have experienced while living with drug addicts. Every individual interprets the data according to their own belief. I give them love and help them to believe that recovery is possible. That's all. What works is their belief in the various mental exercises they do, the bonds that they create, and the therapies I prescribe them. Land is just a positive, non-judgemental space where patients can heal themselves.

Tony, a chronic heroin and methadone abuser from England, came to our centre for treatment in 2006. A few days earlier, he had met a few recovering addicts from Land at his home in Kingsbury. They had finished our rehab programme and were well integrated with their realities in London. They were happy, sober, and living productive lives.

Like Tony, they too had shuffled through several rehabs in England. They seemed to be his doppelgangers. Arrested for petty crimes, many of them exhibited people-pleasing behaviours, had witnessed violence in their families, carried stories of rejection, and were in the habit of stealing from home. These were just a few of their commonalities. One of them was using much higher quantities than Tony had been. They were happy in their recovery. He began to believe that if they could recover, he could too.

The nine months that he spent on Land simply whizzed by, as he did the mental exercises, the physical activities, the therapies and the bonding exercises. He put his heart and soul into everything that was suggested to him. During his tenure at the rehab, he experienced everything that his recovering friends in London had spoken to him about. He developed some good emotional bonds like they did. He took the tenets of the programme seriously as they'd suggested.

Experiencing hundreds of recovering programmers from different countries, with different addictions, strengthened his belief even further. He believed that he could be drug free and happy. More than a decade has passed since then. He is now content and productive, like his mates.

I believe that he had recovered from his traumatic poly drug addiction even before he obtained the boarding pass for his Air India flight from Heathrow to Mumbai. He had decided to quit and believed that he could. The same has been documented over two thousand years ago, as the third of the seven petitions in The Lord's Prayer: 'Thy will be done'.

Whatever anyone believes will be done. His will (decision) was done. Thine will be done, too. All you have to do is believe!

• CHAPTER 19 •

An EVENT THAT DID NOT HAPPEN CHANGED MY LIFE

IT TOOK ME FOUR COLLEGES TO COMPLETE MY FIRST YEAR of undergraduate college. Skipping classes in the fourth one was the only reason why I cleared the term. I simply could not stay put in a classroom without getting into trouble. I would toss chalk and marbles around the class and yell out random words when the professors had their backs turned. My favourite method to irritate my teachers was a devious, well-rehearsed set of answers to any teacher who finished a lecture with the words 'any questions?'

I would keep repeating the same nonsensical sentences. It unfailingly worked—but only once, with every teacher.

Some students would laugh hysterically and I got the 'recognition' I so badly wanted at that time. I would also be scolded and shown the door. Strolling out of the classroom nonchalantly only strengthened my 'image'.

The Q&A sessions would go something like this.

Professor: '…This concludes the chapter on sulphur. Now are there any questions?'

Me: 'Sir, is it raining?'

Professor: 'Why are you asking me this question?'

Me: 'Sir, I live far away and during the rains the tracks get flooded. The trains stop their service and I get stranded.'

Professor: 'It's summer now and it never rains during this season.'

Me: 'Sir, that's why I am asking the question. I know it has never rained during the summer, but if its starts raining this summer, the tracks will still get flooded, the trains will stop their services and I will get stranded.'

Professor: 'But it's SUMMMMMMER.'

Me: 'Sir, that is exactly why I am asking the question. I know it has never rained during the summer, but if it rains now, the tracks will get flooded. Sir, you asked us if we had any questions. This is my question.'

Professor: 'This is a chemistry class—obviously I meant any questions on the subject.'

Me: 'Sir, even if it rains during a chemistry class, the tracks still get flooded. When the tracks get flooded, the trains...'

Professor: 'Get out of my class. RIGHT NOW!'

Most teachers would throw me out of the class at this point. My fellow batch mates would crack up as I made my exit. Every time I strolled out of class, I'd visualise myself as some sort of anti-establishment hero. I had absolutely no self-validation in those days, and desperately sought the validation of others.

My first stop in college was always at the notice board, which carried the names of errant students who were being called to the principal's office. I wanted to be the most notorious guy around. I was disappointed on the days when I didn't make it to the list. Although my deviant behaviour gave me the validation that I needed through the attention of my peers, it also propelled my pseudo-inflated ego to a higher level. This recognition made my conduct even more rebellious. It was a vicious cycle.

Broken blackboards, violent canteen fights, bursting Diwali crackers during lectures, throwing biology specimens around the lab, arguing needlessly with lecturers, flashing a knife once in a while, attempting to kidnap the librarian: these were just some of my shenanigans.

At home things were worse. I would get back early in the morning before my father woke up for his prayers. My grandmother was my enemy as she reported my timings and bad behaviour to him, who would slap or belt me. My mother stayed in her father's home. Ever since I had discovered that she was secretly married to another man, I'd distanced myself from her. She didn't matter to me at all, or at least that's what I wanted to believe.

My boredom threshold was close to zero. I needed excitement all the time. My close friend, Asif Mistry, stood by me through all my messes. Every time he bailed me out, I would promise him that I would never repeat the same mistake. I never broke that promise, I think. I just made new 'mistakes'.

Life was one painful roller-coaster ride with screeching turns that took me down steep slopes of suffering. The unruly behaviour that brought me recognition from my peers pained my near and dear ones. The people who suffered the most were my siblings. The regular reporting of my aberrant behaviour ensured angry and violent scenes at home. The more my father beat me, the more determined I was to break the rules again.

During one of my visits to Asif's home, in my final year at medical school, his grandfather suffered a stroke. The entire household was in panic mode. Asif ran out of the room to call for an ambulance. His father was shouting at everyone around to call the doctor.

I was at his grandfather's bedside. 'Don't worry, Dada, all will be well soon. The doctor is on his way,' I said stroking his hand gently.

He lay on the bed with his left hand gripping his chest, his eyes locked into mine. When he spoke, his voice rasped breathlessly. 'I know that I am going to die...I have been a devout Muslim all my life. I have been praying all five namaaz diligently and have done Haj thrice, but now I am feeling anxious about taking the journey beyond.

'I know that I've been a good Muslim, but that is not helping me. I'm trying hard to recollect all the good that I've done in my lifetime. Remembering my good deeds is giving me some reassurance to set forth on this unknown journey. But for every good deed I recollect, I also recollect a few more bad deeds that I've done.'

He broke into coughs, and his eyes dropped to the floor. When he squeezed my arm lightly, I could feel no warmth from his hands. He whispered slowly, wheezing, long pauses punctuating his sentences, 'Beta...remember when you are at my stage in life, when...you are dying, the only thing... that will matter to you...is how good...you have been. You will also remember the bad deeds...Beta...keep...doing...'

He stopped. I stared at him, worried. He stared back, blankly. He wasn't moving. I freaked out and yelled, 'Asif... Asif...Asif!' I don't remember the sequence of events that followed, though I remember Asif's mother wailing, his brother crying, a doctor and some ambulance boys rushing in. I was more moved than I could express.

Back at my hostel room, I was haunted by his words. They made sense. I decided to concentrate on doing good deeds. I did not want to feel insecure when I was dying.

I stopped baiting my professors and getting into meaningless fights. Over the next few years, I studied at every opportunity I got. After graduating from medical college, I registered for a postgraduate degree in psychiatry. Halfway through that degree, I had a showdown with the head of the department over what I felt was the overuse of electroconvulsive shock therapy. I didn't want to administer ECTs, which were a fundamental part of the treatment in those days.

I changed tack, learning everything I could about drug demand reduction strategies, including drug prevention and drug rehabilitation. Over the next few years I developed a highly successful rehabilitation programme for addicts and alcoholics in the city of Mumbai. I was intentionally doing what I considered good.

My rebellion disappeared once I had established another identity, another goal: that of becoming a good doctor. I wanted to be recognised, but I had acquired another motto: 'Be a good human being.' That was my new mantra.

Over the next decade I moved head-on into achieving my goals. I studied everything I could gather about drug recovery. I met only drug addicts, alcoholics and their families, other experts, as well as film stars and sports celebrities who were part of our prevention campaigns. By then both my parents had died, and my siblings were married and stayed in different parts of the city.

Over time, living with and reaching out to addicts in my home, I too began to transform. The need to seek excitement or validation from others faded away. The angry young man disappeared. Re-examining the past I saw the truth: I cannot hold my parents solely accountable for my actions. I was part of the problem.

My vocation required me to find ways to cut through the distorted perceptions that were part of every addict's world view. As I did that, I also cleared mine.

I was living life on the fast lane. Therapy sessions and prevention campaigns accounted for all my waking hours.

In those early years, I was so closely involved in the process of helping my patients recover that even my brothers and sisters never got to see me.

I would bump into my school friend Asif more than a decade later near his new residence on Residency Road. He invited me home and introduced me to his family. 'This is my best friend from school, Dr Yusuf Merchant.' His sweet daughter, Haya, ran into a bedroom and returned with a scrapbook. Opening the book shyly, she showed me a few clippings from newspapers featuring my photographs with some film stars.

She said in a high-pitched voice, 'My dad would tell me, this celebrity Dr Yusuf Merchant was my best friend all through school and college—I didn't believe him then!'

After treating me to a delicious dinner, Asif saw me to my car. In his characteristic mischievous tone, he inquired, 'Tell me one thing. How come you have changed so much—from that selfish, risk-taking bastard into this good human being and celebrity?'

'It was what your grandfather said,' I told him, the memories rushing back. 'Remember?' I went over that conversation again, telling him in great detail what his grandfather had said to me after he had gone out of the room to phone for an ambulance.

Asif stared at me, dumbstruck. 'Don't fuck around, Yusuf, my grandfather is still alive.'

I was as shocked as he was. But it was Asif saying so; it had to be true. Could I have invented all that had happened? The vivid memories, the visuals, came back to me as I drove back home. Perhaps I had seen his grandfather at a time when he was ill, and had imagined the rest. But it was so real, so clear! Once again, I went over the episode in my head.

I could see myself sitting beside his grandfather. If it

had really happened, I wouldn't be able to see myself in the visual: you don't see images of yourself in recollections of real events. It was a dream, even if it had been an unusually powerful one.

AN EVENT THAT HAD NOT HAPPENED HAD CHANGED THE COURSE OF MY LIFE.

I now believe that the event, and the dream, were both dictated by my intentions. I had wanted to contribute, to make a difference in people's lives ever since my Adyar interaction. (Page 23) My intention to do good must have been so powerful that I dreamt a dream and believed it to be real. Real enough to transform my life into a meaningful one.

The universe finds strange ways to make our intentions come true. Sometimes with events that haven't occurred.

• CHAPTER 20 •

I AM GOING TO DIE!

'I'M SORRY, I CAN'T ISSUE YOUR FATHER A DEATH certificate as I've not seen him during the last three months.'

This was how our family physician, Dr Ramchandani, told me of my father's death.

'I want to talk to you, Bhai,' my father had said to me just twenty minutes earlier. Anticipating one of his prolonged lectures, I'd replied politely, 'I'll come in five minutes, Baba' and had run downstairs for a quick smoke.

Coming back up, I heard my grandmother's loud call, 'See what has happened to Baba!'

I bolted towards his bedroom and was stunned to see him motionless on the floor. I tried to pull him back onto the bed. I noticed that the back of his legs were damp. He was lying in a pool of water.

'Is that urine?' was the fleeting thought. Instinctively, I grasped his wrist to feel his pulse. There was none. His palms were frigid. My head spun as I managed to lift him back on the bed. All my thoughts were incomplete sentences, with the word 'dead' missing. I simply couldn't register that word, and what it meant. My mind speedily substituted other words in place of 'dead'.

'Baba is...very sick.'
'Baba is...needs a doctor.'
'Baba is...call a doctor fast.'
'Baba is...going to be all right soon.'

I could hear disembodied cries: *Kya hua? Baba ko kya*

hua?' Turning around, I saw my grandmother beating her chest repeatedly. She was wailing and telling me that I was a doctor, I could help Baba. She kept pestering me to do something to help him.

'I'm calling Dr Ramchandani,' I shouted back, going into the living room to make the call.

A lot was being said within my hearing range, but in that moment, all I could register were buzzing sounds. I was consumed wholly by the following thoughts:

'Doctor will organise his admission to the Bombay Hospital nearby.'

'I have to take money from the safe to pay the initial deposit at the hospital.'

'I have to call my professors at the J.J. Hospital for a second opinion.'

I grabbed our car keys, pacing up and down between the front door and the door to my father's bedroom. I didn't notice our family physician entering our house.

I first noticed him when Dr Ramachandani appeared out of my dad's bedroom. His hands were buried in the capacious pockets of his white coat. He seemed to be in a hurry to leave. As he walked across the living room, he informed me that he couldn't issue the death certificate. 'What a bastard! Is this how a doctor should break the news of a father's death to his son?' I thought. And then I blacked out.

When I regained consciousness, I was sitting on the floor. Numb. Not a thought in my head. Everything appeared to be still, like I was in a static picture frame. No emotions. Just a photograph of the reality. Then a solitary question flashed through my head, 'What do I do now?' I couldn't speak. I couldn't move.

Even during the period when I resented him, the truth was that my father had been my hero—always. Whenever

I hadn't known what to do, I would always ask myself, 'What would Baba do if he was in my situation?' So now I asked myself, 'What would Baba do if I had died?' The answer rose abruptly, 'Baba would offer namaaz first.'

It had probably been a few years since I had offered namaaz prayers. Quickly I did the requisite ablution, located the prayer mat and closed my bedroom door. I must have prayed for a long time, for when I came out of the bedroom, I saw that the living room was full of people. My grandmother, the neighbours and my patients who lived at home with me were there.

The air felt dense and heavy. My breathing was slow and laborious.

I guess prayer gave me the insight to reach out and ease the suffering of the others present in the room. I saw my grandmother lamenting in a corner. I had lived with my father for twenty-eight years; she had been with him for sixty-three. I let her pain take precedence over mine. Seating myself beside her, I gently held her hands to prevent her from beating her chest. 'Don't beat yourself, Ma. Islam doesn't encourage mourning. Please repeat after me: *Laa ilaaha illal lahu Mohammedur Rasool Ullah.*' I made her repeat the Kalma over and over.

Looking around the room, I noticed the seven addicts who stayed with me. 'These guys are going to learn by observing me. They are going to respond the way I do when their parents die,' I thought to myself. I had to set a good example.

I had two choices. Either I could grieve for the loss of my father or pray for his soul. I chose to pray for his soul. He was a devout Muslim. If he had been alive, he would've liked me to pray. I recited a few prayers that he had helped me memorise.

Then these unsettling questions began to rise up within

me. 'What do I do now? How do we arrange a funeral? Whom should I contact? How do people do this?'

I wasn't a social person and hardly interacted with anyone other than my patients. Then I noticed my neighbour, Mohammad Razzaq. I approached him and requested him to help me with the process. He agreed.

I recollect making only one call. It was to my younger sister, Yasmeen. It was more like a verbal telegram: 'Baba died. Come soon.'

Our living room was now overflowing with people. I didn't recognise most of them. Dad was resting on a bed sheet on the floor, shrouded in a white al-kafan, with some rose petals scattered on his wrapped body. As I didn't smoke in his presence, I stepped outside my main door and lit up.

I knew my father's soul would be happy if I sincerely followed the Muslim rituals for burial. I decided to follow every instruction that Uncle Razzaq gave me without question.

As I stood there in deep thought, I saw two ladies chuckling as they came up the stairs. One of them asked, 'Which one is Adam Merchant's home?' I pointed to the door. In a flash, both of them covered their heads with their dupattas, started bawling loudly and went inside our house. Their histrionics stumped me. 'What was that?' I stood shocked.

Then stubbing out my cigarette, I went in, looking for the two women. I recognised them by their dupattas. I gave one of them a hard tap on the shoulder and shouted, 'Get out now, before I drag you out.' Everyone was startled. As the two women rose hastily, my uncle rushed towards me and said in a whisper, 'Bhai, your grandmother's friends had called them. They are rudali.'

I snarled, 'I don't know what the hell a rudali is, but they have to leave now.'

My uncle put his arm around me and said, 'Rudalis are professional criers. In our community they come to funerals and cry so that others can join in.'

Professional mourners? There would be no farcical dramas at my father's funeral. He was not playing dead. This was not a stage show.

'Get out right now!' I said to the two women again, controlling my voice. As they left, I wondered why I was not shedding tears myself. I just couldn't. There was no way that I was going to fake it. I guessed that I was too shocked to feel my own emotions.

I remember carrying his body to the graveyard. I kept reciting the prayers and asked God to give me the strength to do everything the way my father would have liked me to.

After the funeral prayers at the graveyard, I stepped into the pit with my elder brother, Suleman. Baba's body was gently lowered into it. 'The face should be facing west,' I heard the maulana say. I had no inkling where that was and asked him, 'Which way is west?'

What followed was probably the toughest part of the burial process. I caught a flash of memory: of me, sleeping in Baba's lap when I was very young. He still had the same reassuring smile. Though our roles had been reversed. This time, he was in my lap and I was ruffling his hair.

'God will take care of you,' I felt that that was his last message for me.

I didn't feel any grief even when I returned home—only a huge sense of responsibility towards my siblings. I had to be brave for them. They were in my care now.

I hugged my grieving sisters and told them emphatically: 'Baba's soul is still here and it will pain him to see you crying like this. Let's not be selfish and cry; let us pray for his soul. Our prayers will help him in his journey into afterlife.' I didn't really believe what I was saying, but my father surely had believed in it. I wanted them to believe it as I knew it would prevent them from falling apart.

I was getting progressively irritated with the endless stream of people who walked up to me to say 'Sorry.' 'Why are you saying sorry? Your father is alive. Have you killed him?' I wanted to respond every time. I simply could not comprehend why they kept saying sorry to me or why they were crying. On an impulse, I left and decided to spend some time with my father's body at the graveyard. As I'd thought, I was all by myself at his grave. Being in his proximity comforted me. I fell asleep, praying.

When I woke up, it was dawn. And I was still sitting beside the grave. This was for real. It was not like Asif's grandfather's demise, which had only been a dream. I started praying again until I was interrupted by a group of women and children approaching the grave with buckets full of water.

'Only twenty-five rupees for a bucket of water. If we water the grave, it will give the dead person a cool breeze in heaven. How many should we pour?' said the eldest one, as she hurriedly poured the water in her bucket on the grave.

I was infuriated. First there were professional mourners and now this cool breeze in heaven shit. I thrust a few hundred-rupee notes into her outstretched palm. 'Only one,' I said in a dead voice, and left.

I couldn't go home as there would be the 'sorry' guys there. They didn't even know my Baba that well. I couldn't sit in peace at the graveyard either. I had to go somewhere, be with someone. I decided to go to Warden Road and spend time with my friend, Ankush. On the way I bumped into his friend, Dileep, whom I knew a little.

'You don't look good, Doc. Is everything all right?' he asked.

It took me a while to say the words. 'My father expired.'

He put a sympathetic arm around me and said quietly, 'I know how you feel. My cat died last month.'

I felt good because here was someone who could relate to what I was saying. I felt that he knew exactly how I was feeling. Someone understood my pain.

Later, as I walked back home from Ankush's house, I became fully aware that my father would never be coming home again, but I couldn't detach myself from him. I needed some connection with him. And the best way to establish that connection would be to become the human being he wanted me to be. A simple and honest person who would look after his family.

Earlier, a death that hadn't happened had changed my life and philosophy. This time, a death that had happened was going to make it even more beautiful. I was certain.

The first and last time I cried was ten days later when I experienced a thought that struck me like a thunderbolt: I AM NEVER GOING TO SEE HIM AGAIN. Coping with his death was one thing. Not seeing him ever again was a totally different thing altogether. It was excruciating.

In the next few years, I would encounter death several times. My grandmother, my mother, my sister, my brother and some good friends died, in turn. Each subsequent death was easier to cope with and understand.

About a decade later, when I was walking on the pathway at our rehab centre, I saw our staff member Jaggu performing his routine chore, sweeping the dead leaves off the path. The first thing that I registered was that these leaves dying didn't hurt me. It was followed by thoughts of the 129,000 people who had died and thousands of others who suffered the twin atomic holocausts of Hiroshima and Nagasaki in August 1945.

'It's strange how I am totally unhurt by deaths of people that I am not attached to,' I thought to myself. I realised the true meaning of the thought that all living things die.

All these years I had been forced to contend with death so many times. I'd reached out to the bereaved and prayed for their souls. But not for a single moment had I fully understood that one day I was going to die too. It was another eureka moment of my life.

I AM GOING TO DIE.

I always knew that people die, but I had never actually believed that I was going to. At least I lived as though I'd live forever.

This was the most beautiful realisation I'd ever had.

I am going to die one day.

I decided to enjoy every moment that I lived. I had thirty years (plus or minus a few) more above the ground. Of these thirty, presuming that I continued to sleep for eight hours daily, ten years would be lost in sleep. Another ten years would go at work. I had only ten years to live. Almost instantaneously, I let go of all the hurt and resentments I had been hanging on to. No more extra baggage for me.

Being angry with someone or something for a few weeks in the past had been all right. Not anymore. In the past, I was probably deducting twenty days from infinity. It didn't make any difference at all. I still had infinite years to live. Now I had to deduct twenty days from a finite number, which was less than ten years.

It was not going to happen ever again.

'What would I want to do differently if I died tonight?' I asked myself. There were a host of things that I would do differently. I'd spend more time with my family. I'd try harder to empower people into believing that they could achieve anything. I'd travel around the world. I'd like to share the simple philosophy that my life experiences have taught me—beyond the circle of addicts and their families.

Soon I set the balance right by spending more time with my family, travelling, and empowering people that I met. The last one is fructifying right now as you read this sentence.

• CHAPTER 21 •

The Secret to Self-Confidence

VINITA JUST WON A BEAUTY PAGEANT, ESTABLISHING HER as the most beautiful girl in her college; Shubham is the heir to a billionaire and has always had everything that he demanded for; Larissa has broken the glass ceiling to head an FMCG firm and newspapers have been abuzz with her success story.

One would expect these people to have high self-esteem. They do not. Good looks, professional success or wealth are not necessarily determinants of self-esteem. You could possess all of them and still have low self-esteem.

Many years ago, I had hosted fifty-two episodes of a television show featuring challenged children called *Hamari Duniya* for a national television channel. These children were victims of cancer, blindness or chromosomal defects. The participants included orphans, children from single-parent homes and the like.

In the very first episode, I asked a child who had been blind since birth, 'Who would you like to see first if you get your eyesight?'

He smiled back excitedly, 'God! First I'd like to see God and then my wonderful parents. I would love to see God's beautiful creations.'

I was thunderstruck by the child's positivity. Till then, I had never felt grateful for my own eyes. How could this child be so positive, grateful and happy, I wondered!

Throughout the show, most of the children displayed high levels of maturity and concerned awareness. 'I would like my parents to live their lives happily, they keep worrying about me. Worrying will not cure me; it will only make them unhappy. I have been told that I won't live to see my thirteenth birthday party. What should I do to help my parents stop feeling miserable? I have only three years left,' a ten-year-old patient asked me.

He had thalassemia. His question was so honest, put forward with great confidence. How could he have such a high level of self-worth when he knew that life had been unfair to him? He was subject to painful blood transfusions every fortnight to make up for the deficit of haemoglobin in his blood. He had done nothing to warrant this—it was an inherited disorder. The only wrinkle was that he was the child of a set of parents who had thalassemia minor.

As a doctor I knew that if his parents had only done a special blood test, haemoglobin electrophoresis, before his mother had conceived, the gene could have been identified and this suffering could have been averted easily. Yet, this child experienced his life as a happy one.

The piano recital by a child with Down Syndrome and the art exhibited by another orphan were some of the other highlights of my show. Most of these kids were happy and radiated confidence. They had a positive self-image.

Our sense of self-worth or self-respect is purely mathematical. Add up the total number of your positive experiences and your negative experiences. If the sum is more than zero, you have positive self-esteem. If the number of negative experiences outweigh the positive experiences, you have low self-esteem. The lower the number, the lower the esteem and vice versa.

Of course, there would be a gradation of the experiences. All negative experiences would not account for the same mathematical negative. For a certain woman, an aborted pregnancy might fetch higher negative points than being rejected by a friend; for another woman, it could be the reverse. A parent's praise may add more positive numbers than a friend's praise. But the point is, this number game is constantly playing out in our lives, day in and day out.

Negative self-talk contributes the most to low self-esteem. People who are negative are stuck in a loop of self-deprecating thoughts. The brain accepts all thoughts as real.

People with low self-esteem present themselves in several ways. The snob sitting in a corner displays a pseudo-inflated ego and projects grandiosity. It is a defence mechanism to cover the low self-esteem. The shy girl is riddled with anticipation anxiety caused by predominant thoughts of fear. The depressive is overwhelmed by guilt and seems aloof.

My low self-esteem reflected in the way that I used to mirror people. I would reflect back a version of themselves to the people I met. I thought that that was the only way I would be accepted by others. I didn't really know who I was or what I liked.

Other expressions of poor self-esteem may include fear, hyper vigilance, self-harming behaviours and an array of obsessions.

A girl I knew in college would get a panic attack whenever she spoke to or thought about her ex-boyfriend. They were 'making up' and 'breaking up' for over six months. Every time they separated, her self-regard took a blow. Over a period of time, he had decimated her ego. It was clear to me that she was experiencing self-esteem attacks. I was pretty certain even then that panic attacks are primarily low self-esteem attacks.

'I don't like myself, Baba. I don't like being me,' I remember telling my father during my teen years. I was constantly comparing myself to others.

Baba had said, 'Why don't you go to VT Station at 5.30 p.m. today and observe the people going into the station? More than a million people will be there. Just stand there for an hour, notice as many people as you can, and when you return, tell me who you would like to be. I will try my best to help you become that person.'

At 5.30 p.m. I was there, scanning the crowd to find the person that I wanted to be. I tried hard to get into the skin of some people, first this one and then that one. It took me less than fifteen minutes to understand that I didn't want to be anyone else.

I wanted to be *me*. I wasn't comfortable in my own skin, but I would feel shittier in any other person's body.

I was low on self-confidence. My dad told me that self-confidence was merely the reflection of one's self-esteem. How does one raise one's self-esteem or self-confidence?

Since it's a game of math, you can do so either by decreasing the number of negative experiences in your life or by increasing the positive. To decrease the number of negative experiences, one has to reassess the negative experiences of the past (chapter 16) and stop indulging in negative self-talk. It isn't easy to accomplish. It takes time to train yourself to notice negative thoughts, and deliberately switch your mind to think of good thoughts. It is difficult in the beginning, but it will get easier as you keep repeating positive actions.

Some suggestions to increase self-esteem are listed below:

1. *Maintain a gratitude diary.* In order to be grateful, you will have to shift to a positive state of mind.
2. *Talk kindly to yourself at all times, even when you commit mistakes.* No one is perfect. We all mess up. Don't be afraid to fail. I owe my success to all my failures as I've learnt so much from them.

3. *Surround yourself with positive people.* If you hang out with negative people, you are likely to become more negative.
4. *Pray.* Prayer doesn't change things, but it gives one insight to do the right thing. If I prayed to make my marriage better, it would not become better by magic. I would only get the insight to work on my character defects, be kind and loving to my partner, and honour the relationship. A relationship is like a plant—without constant inputs it withers and dies.
5. *Meditate.* Meditative states produce natural stress busters like endorphins.
6. *Stop comparing yourself with others.* You will feel miserable. One need not look like James Dean or Eva Mendes, or play basketball like Michael Jordan or LeBron James. You don't have to become a legend to feel good about yourself. Focus on what you are good at, and get better at it.
7. *Exercise.* It's not only good for your heart, it's good for your brain too. The metabolites (by-products) of thought also need to be washed away by increased circulation. If you allow them to accumulate, thinking becomes very laborious—any depressive person can vouch for this.
8. *Be mindful of your thoughts.* If you cultivate mindfulness, you can observe your thoughts without reacting to them.
9. *Pat yourself on the back when you do any of the above.* Appreciate your effort. Tell yourself aloud: 'That was a good thing I did. I am in control of my change.'

Finally, *it is only what you think of you that matters.* Only your love for yourself matters. A modern prophet would put it simply, 'Love and respect yourself as you love and respect your neighbours.'

• CHAPTER 22 •

Two Sides to Reality

AT EXACTLY 7.A.M. ON 24 JUNE 2010, A VIOLENT STORM passed through the state of Connecticut. Marlborough, the home town of the Thompsons, who were travelling at the time, received a direct hit. Most of the trees in their neighbourhood were uprooted. A tree crashed directly into their kitchen, ripping open their rear wall.

The Thompsons obviously couldn't hear the sounds of the crash—they were 1600 miles away when it happened. Their closest neighbour, who lived five miles away, did not hear it either.

On their return, the Thompsons were shocked to see the destruction. A part of the ceiling had caved in and their rear wall was totally demolished. Fragments of crockery, glass windows and the marble kitchen counter were strewn in and around what had once been a functional kitchen.

Did the ripping apart of that rear wall, the shattering of glasses and crockery and the splintering of the kitchen counter generate any sounds?

No! No sound ensued. Why?

Simply because there was no one around to hear those sounds.

What if a recording device had been placed at the site of the devastation? Would it record the sounds? No, it would record only the sound vibrations of the destruction. Only if someone were to listen to these recordings would they turn into what we call 'sound'.

The shattering of glasses, ceramics and stone can only create sound waves. To convert these sound waves into sound, one would require the intervention of instruments like our ears and brain.

The sound waves would first vibrate in our eardrums, then in the three connecting bones inside the ear. Eventually, through a series of chain reactions, the vibrations would turn into electrical signals and our brains would then interpret the sounds.

We create all the sounds we hear. Not the objects that apparently make them.

Everything outside our brain, including musical instruments, can only create sound waves, which are potential sound. Our brains convert these potential sounds or waves into sound, provided they lie within the frequency of human hearing.

What about light? Do we also create light? Yes. Our brains create the light, transforming light waves (potential light) into light.

Light behaves like a wave and it also behaves like a particle. There are several simple experiments in physics text books that can easily prove the same. However, this duality collapses into a singular reality in the presence of an observer. The wave properties of light collapse into light particles when an act of observation is made. All of us are powerful, for we are constantly creating our realities.

Any event that happens in your reality is both good and bad at the same time. Holding one perspective makes it appear bad, but you have the power to change it into a different perspective that could be a good one.

The Thompsons were devastated. More than fifty thousand dollars would be required to fix the damage. A new temporary home, near their daughter Jane's current primary school, would have to be found, with the rent being an additional expense. Memories of their travels had been wrecked. Mr Thompson was in a completely negative state of mind. How could this event possibly generate a positive state?

No matter the nature of an event, there is always a dual reality.

Higher exponents of spirituality and quantum physics are aware of this duality. Opposites co-exist and are also the same. For example, hot and cold states are opposites. Yet, they are also the same—both are ranges of temperature.

Is green the colour of life? That is one perspective. Green is the most predominant colour in fields and trillions of trees on our planet. Green algae produce more than 70 per cent of our planet's oxygen. Another perspective is that red is the colour of life. The chlorophyll present in grass, trees and algae absorbs all colour wavelengths, except green. It reflects the unwanted green wavelengths which is why these plants appear to be green in colour. Green is the colour we don't see in dead plants. Dead plants absorb the green. So green should be the colour of death. This is also a correct perspective!

Mr Thompson could change his reality into a positive one. What if they had not been on vacation when the tornado struck their home? He would have been sleeping in his bedroom. His wife and daughter might have been making breakfast in the kitchen when the tree crashed through the wall. From that perspective, a destroyed kitchen was the best-case scenario vis a vis a crippled daughter and wife. The financial losses and inconveniences he has to face now pale in comparison to the loss of human life or severe injuries to his loved ones. 'Thank God we were on vacation! My family is unhurt,' he could then say in gratitude.

Even in my case, the opposition has always persisted. When I had to leave the comfort of my luxurious home and live on the streets, the duality existed. It was both a positive and a negative. At that point in time, I chose to see it as a negative event.

I remember the agony of hunger. It felt as though there was a rat living in my stomach, occasionally gnawing at my insides. Each bite was nerve-racking. No matter how much water I consumed to dilute the naturally occurring hydrochloric acid in my stomach, it didn't help.

A half-rotten banana that I picked up from a garbage bin helped a little. In hindsight I wonder how I didn't find the smell offensive. It was soggy, it tasted delicious.

My father's warning, 'Fishes and guests stink after a few days', came to light sooner than expected. My 'friends', barring Asif, Soeb and Javed, treated me as though I had fish odour syndrome. My presence would cause them to leave in a rush.

I just couldn't control a particular habit, which I now think of as a 'virus line' that would erupt into my conversations. On meeting an acquaintance, my photographic memory would arm me with the names of their siblings and other trivia. I would begin the conversation with 'How are you?' or 'How is your brother?' or 'Which movie did you see last?' Then I would gently lead my potential target to ask questions about my current situation. And, seizing an opportunity, I'd request him to lend me some money.

However, the virus line would simply disrupt the conversation. I would mindlessly rattle off the questions one after the other, not even waiting to receive the answers. The conversation would go something on these lines: 'How are you, how is your brother, which movie have you seen lately, do you have ten bucks???'

I desperately prayed for a well-wisher. I didn't want to be bailed out of my struggle. I just wanted a benefactor who would encourage me and be by my side. I didn't find any. The countless rejections, the insensitivity of others, the loneliness and the humiliation I had to deal with made me extremely miserable and negative.

Today, I see the event as one of the most positive stepping stones I had ever climbed. Not finding a benefactor or well-wisher was the best thing that'd happened to me.

It sensitised me. I became the benefactor that I yearned for. I know exactly what is wanted from a benefactor. Thank God I didn't get one.

No one knew what I wanted better than I did and so I became my own mentor, providing what I once thought I could get only from another person. Becoming what I wanted has made me a wonderful and caring doctor.

Winning a lottery may be a dream for millions. It should be a very positive event. But it isn't.

Most lottery winners become miserable afterwards because they regret spending the money foolishly. The sudden influx of huge amounts of money impairs their judgement. More than half of them go bankrupt.

A positive event could lead to a negative reality and vice versa. We can create any reality out of any event. Sights and sounds. Friends and foes. Pleasures and pains. Chaos and conflicts. Doubts and debts. Triumphs and travails. Beloveds and betrayers. We create them all.

• CHAPTER 23 •

TRANSFORMERS

JIMMY, A YOUTH FROM DOWNTOWN COLABA, MUMBAI, stabbed his mother with a kitchen knife twenty-six times. She bled to death. Her sin? Refusal to give her son money to procure his daily quota of heroin.'

'Ibrahim, a teen from suburban Mumbai, poured kerosene on himself and got burnt alive. Why? Because of the guilt and shame that he had brought upon himself and his innocent parents due to his heroin addiction.'

Narrating a host of real-life incidents that were registered with the Mumbai Police, I deliberately upped the crescendo of my speech. 'Drug deaths are inflicting tremendous suffering on countless families in our country. You can stop a new Jimmy or Ibrahim from germinating in your neighbourhood. Spread the word. Drugs are a crutch that cripple. The time to act is *now*. Tomorrow will be too late. Thank you.'

As anticipated, I received thunderous applause. The churchgoers continued clapping as I took my designated 'Guest of Honour' seat on the stage. Even though the applause was delightful, I was focused on the reaction of the chief guest for the occasion who was seated to my left: Mother Teresa.

She gave me an angelic smile. I felt a flash of pride as I thought, 'She seems to be impressed by my oratory skills.'

The event was a 'Symposium on Drug Addiction' at St Michael's Church in Mumbai. This was the first time I was sharing stage with the renowned Catholic missionary.

The crowd rose to give a standing ovation as the master of ceremonies requested the chief guest to address the gathering. Pushing my chair a few inches more to the left to get a better view, I tilted my face upwards and gazed in admiration. I was all ears. Her first two words were, 'Dr Merchant.' I was in seventh heaven. She had noticed me!

But by the time she'd completed the sentence, I felt like a shithead. The sentence was, 'Dr Merchant spoke about a boy who'd killed his mother—we must love the boy.' She then continued, 'We must hug the boy. The poor boy needed love. Love is the answer.' The next thirty minutes were all about love and forgiveness.

On my way back home, I was a transformed man. The purpose of my speech had been to impress Mother Theresa and the gathering. On earlier occasions, too, my speeches were aimed at bowling out audiences with my eloquence.

But, the solution was different. Where I could see drama, she could see love. Only love. Or its absence. Only the truth.

Since then, my intention has been to communicate with audiences—for their betterment, not for accolades.

The first rehearsed speech I had given was to my father. I was just ten years old then. My mother would regularly list out a list of grievances that my father was inflicting upon her. She would almost always sob and tell us that she couldn't bear the suffering anymore. She was going to kill herself to end the misery. It was an after-school ritual that ended the moment the doorbell announced his return.

I wanted to confront my Dad, and I frequently rehearsed the sentences in my mind, working on different tone scales for the desired effect. But when I finally had the opportunity, I would simply chicken out.

One day, as soon as he woke up from his afternoon nap, I impulsively launched into my rehearsed diatribe.

'Baba, you are a horrible person. Why do you hurt my

mother so much? Instead of praying in the masjid, why don't you actually become a good Muslim and treat her with respect? Aren't you ashamed of your behaviour? I don't care if you aren't. Don't you dare strike her again…'

I was expecting him to yell at me and start hitting me. I wanted him to kill me and go to jail. That would free my mother from the routine torture. My intention was to instigate him to commit homicide.

I had planned to end my tirade with 'Kill me bastard if you care for your life. If you don't, then I am going to stab you in your sleep.' But I abruptly ended at 'Kill me…' I just couldn't go any further.

Then I noticed my Baba crying. His head was high, his arms were folded across his chest. His face was expressionless, but tears flowed down his cheeks.

I ran out of steam. My vision drifted to the bedpost. His response was a novelty. Baffling.

'Bhai, have you finished, or is there more?' I stood there, paralysed. His politeness, even through his tears, was agonising.

'Go on. Please tell me everything that you wanted to,' he said gently, still weeping. Blood was gushing through the veins in my limbs, making me tremble. I could hear my heart beating. Only the bedpost was in focus. I felt dizzy and thought I'd collapse on the floor.

'Look at me,' my father said. I risked a quick upward glance. He unclenched his hands, wiped his tears, took a deep breath and stared back at me.

I felt like my dad was Robert De Niro, looking through the lens attached to his rifle in *Deer Hunter*. I was the deer. I wanted him to take his 'one shot' quickly. I wanted the bullet to graze the carotid artery in my neck, ensuring a bloody and painful and slow death. I deserved the worst.

A few agonising seconds later, he pulled the trigger.

'Bhai, even a murderer gets a fair trial in a court of law before being hanged. You have hanged me without seeking my version of the truth, haven't you?'

A sense of shame started to come over me. I didn't know how I had wronged him, but I was certain that I had never seen him cry before. Not even once. Why didn't I think of asking him for his version of the story?

'Bhai, for this I should punish you. Do you agree?' he said with gentle dignity. I was ready for any retribution. It was warranted. I was hoping that the penalty would be harsh and painful. Just cutting off my tongue with a rusty knife wouldn't do it justice.

'You know what the punishment is? The punishment is that I will never tell you the truth. Please leave the room now.' He pointed towards the door.

Many years later, when I eventually realised the terrible hurt that I'd inflicted on him at that time, it transformed me into a non-judgemental person. I wouldn't do this to anyone again, ever!

This transformation has made me a better human being and therapist. I do not pass judgements easily. Not even after giving a fair hearing to both sides in an argument. I only offer love to both the bearers of conflicting perspectives.

What about the people who hurt or betray me? Earlier, I would get anxious and upset for a while. But not anymore. I feel that people have their own warped reasons for doing what they do. It's all right. They couldn't have behaved differently at that moment anyway.

If it was possible for us to rewind time and relive our past all over again, it would give us the opportunity to do many things differently. We could circumvent failures and pain. But I am sure that it wouldn't be worth the effort. For it would rob us of our motivation and evolution.

One of my prominent failures was my first public drug

The littlest things become powerful sources of joy, meaning, beauty and lessons to my life, when i can remember to notice and enjoy them. My audacious experiments and beautiful failures, thank you ✶

awareness rally. It was intended for an expected crowd of more than ten thousand people at the Cooperage football grounds. The film star Sunil Dutt had agreed to deliver the keynote address. Several hoardings in Mumbai displayed the details, and we had splashed advertisements in leading newspapers.

As I walked alongside Mr Dutt into the football stadium, I expected deafening cheers to soon erupt all over the sprawling grounds. Then I saw the microphone shining under the stadium lights. I was stunned.

In that huge stadium, there were just seven people, including Mr Dutt and myself. I felt hugely embarrassed and turned to Mr Dutt. 'Sorry, Mr Dutt. I really thought the gathering would be large.'

'Don't worry, Dr Merchant,' he smiled. Putting his arm around my shoulder, he continued, 'It shows why we need to have public talks like this. Nobody gives a damn about drugs. They think it won't happen in their homes. In one of my films I had uttered some lines, which seem most appropriate for you in this moment.' Clearing his throat, he put on his filmy voice, *'Main akela ja raha tha janvi manzil magar, log aate gaye, caravan banta gaya.* Dr Merchant, it means: I was travelling alone to a known destination. People kept joining the bandwagon. Just keep heading to your destination. I promise, people will keep joining your mission. All big movements have begun like this. Small. Even during the movement for Independence, Mahatma Gandhi started with a handful of people.'

Mr Dutt had accompanied me to several colleges in Mumbai earlier. He had spoken to halls packed with college students for about fifteen minutes each time. This time, he spoke for an hour and a half—to five people!

More than his filmy dialogue, his resolve stirred my motivation. And I found a friend and a mentor. What a beautiful failure! I wouldn't trade it for anything in the world.

For the next decade, Mr Dutt accompanied me all over India. In 1988, he marched for peace against the atomic bomb, from Hiroshima to Nagasaki. When he returned from his peace march in Japan, he transformed me again. With a cup of tea that he prepared and served me.

He was demonstrating the Zen art of tea making and serving, putting all his love into every movement of the process. The gentle pouring of the tea into a cup. The delicate addition of the sugar. The slow, deliberate swan-like action to stir the sugar. Even the love and affection in handing me the cup was palpable. 'Dr Merchant, we can enjoy every moment we live. In everything we do. E N J O Y.'

He had changed me once again. I decided to put the word to use. 'Enjoy the drive back home,' I thought to myself. What a beautiful ride it was. I had followed the same route over a hundred times before. But just being aware of one word—'enjoy'—transformed it into a beautiful one.

You can experience the power of the word 'enjoy' with this little experiment that you can do right now.

Look at five things that are around you. Each for about three seconds each. Any object to your left, to your right, up, down and then this book. Now repeat the same sequence, but this time bearing in mind the word 'enjoy'. Don't just say the word in your mind. Mean the word. Remind yourself to enjoy looking at the same objects in the same sequence.

I bet the second time was so much more beautiful.

Enjoy! Transform.

• CHAPTER 24 •

the EVENTUAL REALITY

MORE THAN A HUNDRED TOURISTS ARE HUDDLED ON THE steps leading to the majestic Basilique du Sacre-Coeur in Paris. The haunting melody of Beethoven's *Moonlight Sonata*, played on a harp, is slowly enveloping the crowd in a trance-like spell. The beautiful Paris skyline accentuates the harpist's form, playing as though he's conducting a ballet, his graceful fingers dancing lightly across the strings.

Two attractive Serbian teenage girls cut a purposeful swathe through the seated crowd. When their deliberate disruption makes any of the tourists look in their direction, that person is greeted with a fake smile and an outstretched hand holding a rose. 'Only one euro,' the girls recite, almost in unison.

Ambika Nayak, a young musician from India spellbound by Beethoven, loses her concentration. She makes a small sound of annoyance, and looks away resolutely.

Marc Roberts retreats from the duo, jutting his lower lip out unconsciously, as his hand goes protectively to cover his left coat pocket. He had been pickpocketed at the Trocadero metro station on his way to the Eiffel Tower just the day before.

Julian and David, teenagers as well, start smoothening their jeans, squaring their shoulders to show off their pecs. They stand up, sensing opportunity.

Mr Adongo gets teary-eyed. The girls bring back memories of his wife, the way she had lovingly tended the little rose garden in their backyard when she was alive.

Balachandran is slowly sizing the girls up, drawn by the whiteness of their skin. Playing with the ring on his finger he doesn't notice that he's shaking his head from side to side, displaying discomfort. He decides to buy some whitening skin cream before he goes back to his native place, Hyderabad.

Mr Johnson smiles at the girls and buys the rose. One of the Serbian teens reminds him of his daughter, Charlotte. It's been two years since she died in a motorbike accident.

The same incident, the appearance of two girls with a flower, generates such diverse responses, creating dissimilar realities.

Let us follow the sequence of happenings in Mr Johnson's brain to understand how an event turns into a reality.

When Mr Johnson first sees the teens with the rose, the visual and audio data streams enter his brain via his eyes and ears. It takes Mr Johnson a mere one ten-thousandth of a second to register these impulses.

The brain is primarily a pattern cognisance machine. In the next hundredth of a second, the brain scans its data base and matches the patterns it has just received to similar patterns in the past. His synaptic signals are buzzing with nerves firing 200 times every second at an acceleration of 100 metres per second. Mr Johnson's brain finds a match with Charlotte. Data files connected to Charlotte are emerging— zapping from his memory database at super speed.

The data churns out a train of thought.

'If Charlotte was alive today, she would've been here with me. Her endearing smile. God! The accident. If only she had not been friendly with that asshole who took her for a ride. She gifted me a rose on her fifteenth birthday. We were the best father–daughter duo. Her smashed skull. How can God be so cruel? She is no more!'

In the next ten-thousandth of a second, an avalanche of

chemicals from Mr Johnson's brain releases neurotransmitters into his bloodstream electrically. His endocrine system goes into over drive, releasing hormones in a jiffy. Mr Johnson is now experiencing a sad, melancholic feeling. The feeling has created a depressing reality.

It takes less than half a second from the entry point of the data into Mr Johnson's brain to create a depressing reality.

Like Mr Johnson, our realities are carved out by conditions within our brains. Our reality does not hinge on external circumstances. It depends on our perceptions of those circumstances. (Our perceptions are controlled by a few bits of matching patterns that spring forth from our brain database. The data stored is almost impossible to compute. Our brains are exposed to two million bits of data every second. This transpires to 130 million bits every minute or 7.8 billion bits per hour or 187.2 billion bits of data every day of our lives.)

It is impossible for the brain to scan its entire database. What filters the match is our attention.

All my mother's actions were perceived by me as fraudulent simply because I couldn't let go of the fact that she'd 'cheated' me. Any action she took was viewed through a 'cheater' filter in my brain and turned into a negative reality. Even events that were explicitly good for me turned into deceiving and detrimental realities.

I was growing exponentially miserable, for the 'cheated' filter only guaranteed a string of pathological relationships when I had emotional involvements with women. Invariably, sooner or later, I would find a match with some of the negative patterns that matched with my mother's.

A rule was created by me at the age of thirteen: DO NOT THINK ABOUT MOM.

I didn't know then that the rule only ensured that I would keep thinking about her. Brains do not like threat responses and have to be on constant vigil for any threat in order to protect us. The rule merely confirmed my mom was a threat. This assured my brain that in order for it to protect me from Mom, it had to keep a watchful eye for similar patterns.

My mother had her own reasons for keeping her divorce and second marriage a secret from her children. It was only when I understood her reasoning that it became possible for me to genuinely forgive her. When I did that, the threat no longer existed. There was only love. My brain would now perceive future patterns it received that matched my mother's as positive ones.

Our realities only further strengthen our beliefs. Our beliefs reinforce the events in our lives by precipitating behaviours that are consistent with our beliefs. This further contributes to the external events that caused our original negative reality. The dreadful cycle continues.

Pablo from Puerto Rico has been insecure about his relationships ever since his parents separated. His belief that he would be friendless distanced him from his classmates. On occasions, when the other children demonstrated affection, he would push them away by responding in an overbearing manner. Pablo was not aware that it was his response that was pushing his schoolmates away.

The love of his life, Rachel, grew sick of him within the second week of their relationship. It barely survived a month. She experienced him as a very possessive and dominating guy. His belief that 'she will leave me' guided his behaviour. Any man she spoke to was perceived as a potential threat.

In order not to lose her, he insisted that she spend all her free time with him. Even after school hours.

She was swiftly 'creeped out' by the frequency of his calls and emails. It was harrowing for her to deal with

i have been the proverbial blind man to the grand elephant of my life. There's so much more to everything around me than the scant 'reality' of my perception Discarding old beliefs and fears now, i'm discovering what a huge world of possibility there is – has always been – within my reach ✷

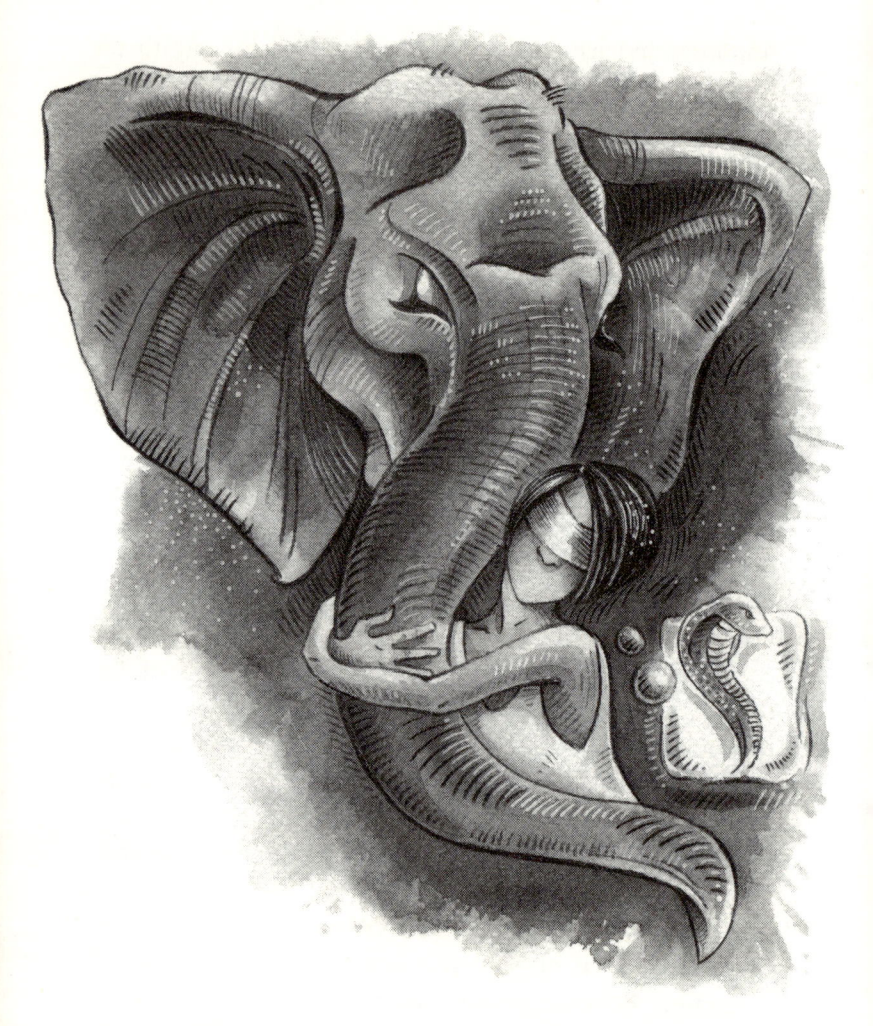

his overreactions if there was a delay in her replies to his messages or a perceived 'wrong' tone of speech. The breakup was painful and traumatic for Pablo. He insisted that his girlfriend, Rachel, was responsible for 'destroying' his life—totally oblivious that it was his behaviour that had caused the damage. A behaviour that stemmed from his own belief system.

Like Pablo, all of us are like hooked fish. Trapped in the barb of our own negative beliefs.

The good thing about negative beliefs is that you can squash them easily. Just think of a few occasions when your negative belief was proved untrue. Whoosh! It will become less powerful. Keep repeating the process and within a few days it will be gone.

Perceptions of events and our responses to them determine the course of our lives. Adverse events will keep occurring, in our homes and in our environment. No one can control any event, but everyone can control the way it is perceived—thus everyone can control their realities.

An event may cause pain but it's the way we perceive it that will decide whether it transforms into suffering or not. Grab the wheel.

༄

• CHAPTER 25 •

the COMMITMENT FUNDA

THREE FEET OF RAINFALL IN A SINGLE DAY. THAT'S WHAT happened when clouds burst over Mumbai on 26 July 2005. The subsequent deluge resulted in a total disruption of train services and an unparalleled traffic jam in the city. Low-lying areas were completely submerged. The suburban electric supply was disconnected, plunging a large part of the city into darkness.

The flood situation kept worsening gradually. 150,000 commuters were stranded on the roads or on trains. More than a hundred people died trapped in their luxury motor vehicles which shut themselves off—computerised vehicles have a mind of their own. When they sense danger, they lock down completely. The imprisoned passengers couldn't break open the glass windows. They asphyxiated due to the increasing carbon dioxide in the enclosed spaces within the sealed cars.

The rains continued through the next day, coinciding with my scheduled visit to our rehabilitation centre. My driver, Rafiq, and I left for the rehab. We had, on several occasions in the past, trudged through floods in Mumbai, in our SUV, patiently weaving through stalled vehicles. But just fifteen minutes into the journey, we realised that this was not a normal monsoon downpour.

Taking the wheel from Rafiq, I plodded on in low gear. The technique, I remember, was to keep my foot on the accelerator and apply pressure. It prevented the water from back-pedalling into the carburettor. If water got into it, the engine would be silenced, and we would come to a halt. I had to reach the rehab facility somehow.

The forty-mile distance usually takes about an hour and fifteen minutes during peak traffic hours. That day, six hours later, we had passed Kalyan city, still some distance from the centre. Rafiq and I had planned the detour through Kalyan—our usual route was jam-packed with vehicles stalled in knee-deep water.

Within the next fifteen minutes, I braked. Our SUV had almost gone into a huge cavity that'd opened up right before our eyes. Water rushed into the trench with the force of a miniature waterfall—even a V8 powered Land Cruiser with its 381 HP wouldn't stand a chance. The road had been washed away.

The locals told us that the authorities had opened the Barvi dam gates the previous evening, and the water level at the site was much higher than its current knee-high swirling presence. The levels had been rapidly receding since morning to its current state.

I got down from the car, asked Rafiq to guard it, and decided to tackle the remaining six miles by foot.

In my school days, floods were an awful lot of fun. We loved wading through the water, splashing it on innocent passers-by. I enjoyed getting wet in the rain. Dragging my friends into the water was just pure entertainment.

Getting through the trench was rough, since the current was almost as strong as you'd find in a whirlpool. The copious rains pelted down upon me and the strong headwinds turned the raindrops into hard spikes of water that stung when they landed on my skin. The rain came down relentlessly, sometimes blinding me. The setting promised a perfect adventure.

Wading through the water, I saw smaller cars wobbling

gently as I passed them. I almost walked into the carcass of a dead animal, but it was carried away by the current. Every step that I took was measured, as the roads were riddled with potholes. I fully enjoyed every moment of the danger. My awareness was heightened. I was in damage control mode.

I wasn't thinking of the rain. My mind was replaying a boxing match, the bantamweight finals of the Western India Championship. In those days, all boxers were inspired by Mohammad Ali, the reigning heavyweight champion, known for his psychological tactics. My opponent was a sturdy Iranian, who had advanced into the finals after successive knockouts. As we shook hands he snarled, his lips tightly and menacingly curled into 'T.K.O.' Technical Knock Out.

'No way!' I retorted, masking my fear.

It was a pretty one-sided contest. I was bobbing and weaving through the bout. He was punching and pawing. Towards the end of the first round he surprised me with a corkscrew punch. The force of the blow dazzled me. I was saved by the bell.

The next round saw me rolling his punches. He connected six times to my head. I was no glass jaw. I constantly stared into his eyes, while deflecting his blows. One wild liver shot took me down to the floor again. When I got up, he unleashed a flurry of shots. I could only see a blur. The bell rang.

As I sat down in my corner, my chief second advised me to throw in the towel. Forcing a smile, I replied, 'No way, I'm fine. I'll get him.'

As we centred for the final round, I screamed, 'What happened to your T.K.O., asshole?' Within the first thirty seconds, I connected a right jab and followed it up with a forceful left hook. He stumbled backwards, but regained his posture and hit back with a haymaker. I was knocked down.

The referee started the eight counts. 1…2…3…4…5—and then I was standing again.

This happened thrice during the round. One of his uppercuts had cut a gash above my left eye. I couldn't see anything. I was holding my hands up to parry the shots to my face and protect my upper abdomen.

For the last, never-ending thirty seconds, I was on the ropes. He was going mad, throwing his wild punches randomly. The pain was excruciating. My head was spinning. I twirled my left hand in the ropes to prevent myself from falling down again. I was just chanting a mantra in my semi-conscious state, 'No T.K.O.' Every punch that I received, I repeated the mantra in my mind.

Finally, the bell rang.

My chief second rushed and placed a large chunk of ice wrapped in a towel on my bleeding eye. As the referee raised my opponent's hand and declared him the winner, I bent forward to meet his eye. 'T.K.O.?' I asked the Iranian, waving my right glove between our faces.

I thought to myself, 'When Bhai decides to do something, he always does it. Nothing has ever stopped him.' It didn't matter when I reached my destination. I was certain of one thing—somehow I would reach there.

Seven delightfully laborious hours later, I reached the gates of the rehab and tugged at the rope attached to the bell. The sense of fulfilment I felt cannot be expressed in words. I felt proud of myself for I had honoured my commitment. What a great feeling!

Was I inconvenienced? I don't really remember. Perhaps I was inconvenienced, but I loved every moment of it. Commitment is a value I hold dearly. Thank God I made that commitment. My values made this journey to our rehab so beautiful.

I often tell my boys and girls in therapy sessions,

'Values are tested by inconvenience. The more troublesome the inconvenience, the more you enjoy holding on to the value.' I understood the same, experientially, once again.

Till the time I was in my teens, I did not value anything. Not even myself. I would often engage in death-defying stunts. Running on top of moving trains. Hanging off cliffs. Driving recklessly. Anything that promised me a buzz and took my attention off myself irrespective of the danger involved.

I constantly needed to distract me from myself. I had zero self-esteem, and it was souring my life. My perceptions were achingly distorted. Almost anything anybody did either angered or hurt me. My perceptions were merely a derivative of my needs. My needs themselves were governed by my values. I valued the validation of others around me as I didn't possess any self-validation.

I didn't really know who I was. I only mirrored others. So many fake selves were created to please different people. Even if I had held on to a single positive value, my needs would have been different, as would my perceptions, beliefs and behaviours.

What are values? They are self-chosen virtues in perpetuity.

How does one inculcate a value? It's pretty simple. Adopt a virtue and stick to it forever. If you want 'family' to be a value, decide to make it a value and continue to hang on to it till you die.

It doesn't matter if you didn't value your family just a minute ago. From now on, it is a value.

Commitment was not a value to me until I met Mr Amitabh Bachchan, the legendary Bollywood actor. My friend, Nana Chudasama, had organised a function at St Xavier's college in Mumbai. Those days, we were constantly staging anti-drug programmes with film stars. We had learnt to call celebrities who had confirmed their participation at least two hours prior to the required time.

The function was to start at 9 p.m. sharp. Mr Bachchan was requested to reach the venue at 7 p.m. He was the biggest star of them all. Since lesser celebs were fashionably late, we assumed that he would be late too. I had calculated that if he was two hours late, he would still be exactly on time.

While I was organising the seating arrangements, some volunteers rushed in, startled: 'Amitabh Bachchan is here!' I glanced at my wrist watch. It was 6.59 p.m.

I don't know what shocked me more, my embarrassment or the timing of his arrival. Noticing my awkwardness, he smiled to put me at ease. He sat down on a plastic chair in the audience section and in his usual baritone asked, *'Cutting chai milegi?'*

He shook my hand firmly and casually informed me that since he had committed to fifteen minutes he would leave at 7.15 p.m. I was amazed by his humble and gracious demeanour. To cover my embarrassment, I started briefing him about the drug problem in India. He listened, and when fifteen minutes had passed, he said, 'Thank you, Dr Merchant', and waved goodbye.

Later, I learnt from other celebrities that Mr Bachchan never delayed on a commitment. He was like a German precision machine—on time, all the time.

Wow! That was so cool. I experienced commitment as a value for the first time. And decided that henceforth I would be too. I do not commit easily, but when I do, I never break it. Since that day.

As I grew older, I accumulated several values. Meaningful relationships, work, family, integrity, love, gratitude, empathy and prayer—to list a few notable ones. The longer the list grew, the more meaningful my life became.

Adding gratitude to the list made me positive by default. No matter how unfavourable an event was, I never let go of gratitude. The 'Why me, God?' days were over and the 'Thank God, it's me!' days began.

Whenever people betrayed or hurt me, I thanked God first. Then I introspected for a reason to thank God. Invariably, I always found a valid reason. It has either helped me to evolve or has been good for me.

This understanding has never happened at the impact point, but a few days or weeks later. Every single time.

I value being a good human being. What if I decide to give a three-day break to this value? The time would be more than sufficient to take out my anger on a few guys who have been messing with my family. After three days, I could go back to upholding my value—to be a good human being.

Many a time, I've been seriously tempted to react violently to people who have tried to harm me or my family. I never have.

If I had, it would only mean that I never valued being a good human being in the first place. For values are self-chosen virtues in perpetuity. There could be no break in their constancy. Any break in a virtue would mean the absence of that value.

Alcoholics and drug addicts can testify the relationship between value and inconvenience. The more they are inconvenienced to get their value (drug of choice), the more they enjoy the substance.

7.5 million people, more than the entire population of New Zealand, travel packed like sardines in Mumbai trains daily. They work in Mumbai's commercial district. Most of the commuters have to spend over an hour standing and smelling the sweat and armpits of their co-passengers as they hang on to the grab handles on their long commutes. Why? Because they value their jobs and families.

Adopt a few values of your choice today. They will enhance your life. Honest!

• CHAPTER 26 •

Les GRANDS MANUELS

ONE OF THE MOST INFLUENTIAL JOBS IN THE WORLD REQUIRES no qualification. All you need is an active sexual organ and healthy accessories in your reproductive system. You have to merely copulate with the opposite sex. That's it! When one out of the 200 million odd sperms penetrates the ovum, the interview is egged. You get the job, roughly nine months later. You become a parent. You immediately qualify to run a P-911, a parent hotline for any emergency.

For the vast majority, parenthood is a self-taught specialty, learnt by trial and error. The knowledge available for reference is restricted to the new parent's own perceptions of parenting when he/she was a child. Imagine the chaos if engineers, doctors, chefs, pilots or other professionals used this learn-on-the-go method to master their occupations?

'You should get up early. Don't you know that the early bird gets the first worm!' my mom would shout as she shook me up from my deep sleep.

I was sleepy and cross. 'What if I'm the early worm? I'll be caught. Relax, Mom, today is a Sund…', but before I could complete the sentence, I got a tight slap.

'You should get up early because I say so' was her uncompromising reply.

This 'because I say so' thing didn't ever make any sense to me. I don't think it does to anybody—child or adult. There is no doubt that she wanted me to rise early because she loved me and wanted me to be a disciplined child. But the

i am a child of the Universe — a manifestation of the earth's joy for itself — brought forth into living through you. Unflinchingly, with all my heart, i place my spirit and trust in your hands. All i ask is: please hold lightly *

manner in which she expressed herself masked that love. I didn't see it; I only felt her anger and the stinging sensation on my cheek. She was not an exceptionally negative person; she was just a regular mother.

Parents can and should learn from the law. In a court of law not only should justice be done, it should also be evident that justice is done. When a judge and jury sentence an accused to long years in prison, you won't hear them saying in court, 'Because I say so.' The sentences are supported by a ruling, an exhaustive document explaining their reasons.

Communicating the reasons for decisions will help children understand their parents' opinions and restrictions. For many parents, a recurring theme is, 'I would never do a thing like this.' It agitates them when their children do things that they would never do. They can't accept it. A suggestion for these types of parents is a simple twenty-second visualisation exercise.

1. Close your eyes.
2. Visualise yourself and your child joined by the umbilical chord. Enjoy the feeling.
3. Sever the chord in your mind.
4. See you and your child as separate entities.

Your child is not you, will not be you, and cannot be you. She or he is another human being.

Physical violence, no matter how minor, should be avoided. For all children, parents are their principal protectors. When the protector turns into an oppressor, the child gets separated not only from the oppressor, but also from him/herself. They want the parent to protect them even while the same parent is being hurtful. The person who is supposed to protect them from harm is harming them.

Are parents conscious of this fact? Are they aware that

apologising for their mistakes later doesn't cement the wedge created in the child's mind? When a vase breaks, it breaks. Even if it is glued back together well, cracks will show.

'You idiot, you can never get things right,' the child will say and mentally admonish himself. Probably exactly in the same way that his parents did when he was young. He will nurture himself the way his parents reared him for the rest of his life. His children, too, will be parented in the same way. This may explain why battered children so often grow up to become battering adults. Nurture children with kindness and love and they will do the same to others for all the days of their lives.

Parents often shout or beat their children for doing wrongful actions. In case of repeat performances, they rerun the same strategy more ferociously. If anger doesn't work, they get angrier. If shouting doesn't work, they shout harder. Repeating the same strategy gets the same undesired result.

The smart thing to do would be to change strategy. Shifting to a loving strategy and seeing the difference. Love is the most powerful force in the universe.

The child wants the parent's attention and is going to obtain it by hook or by crook. If the parent doesn't give her positive attention, she will seek out negative attention through 'bad' behaviours. Children reiterate behaviours that are noticed. Notice the good in your child and see them replicate the good actions.

Dolphin trainers can coach dolphins to do spectacular acrobatics, play ball, and even jump through circlets. They don't beat the aquatic mammals into submission. They don't even speak the language of the dolphins. How do they succeed? They merely notice and reward the dolphins that do the intended actions correctly. Over and over. Taking baby steps at a time, the dolphins learn to do very complicated tasks.

On rare occasions, my father would ask God to forgive him for giving birth to a snake like me, '*Tauba, tauba tauba, maine no saap ko janam diya hai. Ya Allah mujhe maaf kardo*'.

Before he uttered these words, I would always be subjected to a violent thrashing. It didn't make even a dent in my deviant behaviour. (Just for the record, I'd like to add that my instigation and confrontational skills were exemplary. He was not violent, even once, with any of my other four siblings.)

Because I didn't get enough positive attention from my father, I used his cars and splurged his cash to get it from my 'friends' outside. In those days, people would smoke '555' cigarettes. Each pack would cost six rupees. Every time I bought a pack, I would give a hundred-rupee note to a 'friend'. Taking only the '555' packet from him, I'd arrogantly ask him to keep the change. I'd try to buy friends. I didn't make any real ones, but I certainly got their positive attention. Lots of it.

My father's threat, 'You will come home by sunset or face my anger', was matched by thoughts in my head, 'Let's see who comes home before sunrise.' Even if I didn't have friends to hang out with, I would spend the time on my own. Those times were extremely boring, but there was no chance I'd return before sunrise.

However, when my father grew sick of my shenanigans and started ignoring me, I felt worse. He stopped paying attention to my anti-authority behaviours. When we were at the dining table, he would joke with everyone else, pretending that I was absent at the table. He would look through me, failing to acknowledge my presence in the room. I simply couldn't bear the exclusion and very soon fell in line.

'No attention' hurts more than 'negative attention'.

Every action taken by a parent is recorded for posterity. 'This hit you. Huh?' I've seen many parents say as they slap the floor in response to a toddler falling. Smack! Smack! Smack! After a few smacks on the floor, the toddler stops crying. The parent is relieved.

However, the child has also, inadvertently, learnt to blame the floor for the fall. He has learnt to blame—a curse that will handicap him through his life. It's like a plague that will make him desperately seek out others to blame for his failures. Every human being is accountable for his or her own actions. This child will not believe this. He or she will search for external reasons all the time.

Learning the blame game is detrimental for the child. *Blame only ensures that a solution can never be found for a problem since the solution lies outside the person, in another body.*

My father taught me several good things. One of the biggest gifts he gave me was teaching me to celebrate failure. When I lost my first boxing bout, my father informed me that we were going to celebrate it. He bought me some clothes and treated me to a sumptuous dinner at the Taj Mahal Intercontinental, a five-star hotel.

'Bhai, life is full of failures and successes. You have to be brave in both situations. Trust me, it is easier to be brave in failure than in success. Success requires more courage. You love Sunil Gavaskar, right? He is a cricketing legend. He also gets out for a duck, doesn't he? But he makes a comeback with a century soon enough. No one wins all the time. Celebrate your failures too. Life is such.'

Children learn through observation. They don't pay much attention to what their parents say. They learn from observing their parent's actions. When I was sixteen, there was a major fire in my dad's warehouse. I went to the site to inspect the damage. The godown's stocks had burnt and the entire inventory was in ashes.

I rushed to tell my dad of the calamity. He asked me if I had seen the burnt warehouse. I said I had, looking at the floor in dejection. 'Cheer up, Bhai. We are alive. It's all right. Life is such,' he winked through a weak smile. I was taken aback by his response for a few moments. Then I, too, smiled.

The learning was stamped, sealed and registered. 'It's all right to fail.'

By the time parents fully perfect the art of parenting, their children have grown up and become adults. That's why when they get the chance to play parents to children again, they are revered and referred to as grandparents. It's a good way to celebrate what they have finally learned.

IV. STARTING OVER

training the mind

CHAPTER 27

DRUGS, ALCOHOL and ALL THAT BUZZ

UNDERSTAND JUST TWO WORDS. UNDERSTAND ADDICTION. To develop a better insight into the secretive and seductive world of addiction and its treatment, we have to understand just two words.

The words are *High* and *Joint*.

What is a high?

Drug addicts (substance abusers) use various drugs to get a high. Uppers and downers both give them a high. Stimulants like cannabis, cocaine, ice, M-CAT and other amphetamine analogues make them experience a high. Depressants of the CNS (central nervous system) like heroin, sedatives and tranquilisers also produce a high. Alcohol, a drug in liquid form, is also a CNS depressant that gives a high.

Any substance that has a potential for abuse can induce a high. Glue, petrol, snake bites also have the same effect. LSD (lysergic acid diethylamide) was a drug created to study the efficacy of antipsychotics on animals. It induces psychosis. This induced psychosis is also experienced by users as a high.

A High Is Any Place That Is Not Here.

An addict acutely wants to get away from where she or he is. S/he is uncomfortable in her or his *here* (reality). Any place other than 'here' is a safe place.

Treatments that merely concentrate on decoupling an addict from his substance will not be effective. In aversion therapy, the alcoholic is given disulfiram (antabuse), and then forced to drink a few millilitres of alcohol to induce extreme discomfort. Disulfiram blocks the metabolism of alcohol at the acetaldehyde level and symptoms of acetaldehyde poisoning like flushing, breathing difficulties, nausea and vomiting occur. Over a few weeks the alcoholic is supposed to develop a strong aversion to alcohol. This method almost always fails as the drinker still lives in a negative reality, and his or her basic problem remains unaddressed.

In order to have a positive outcome, a treatment process has to assist in making the *here* of the addict comfortable. For users, alcohol or drugs are *solutions*. Rehabs need to find the problems of the addicts and help them fix those. To get them comfortable in the *here*. Rehabs will need revolving doors until they sort this out. Alcohol, drugs or peanuts are not intrinsically harmful substances. Some people experience a severe drop in blood pressure and can get a cardiac arrest if they eat peanuts. People allergic to peanuts can even die due to anaphylaxis.

Addictive personalities are similarly allergic to addictive substances. Everyone who drinks alcohol doesn't become an alcoholic and ruin his life. Statistics reveal that only two out of ten people who drink alcohol regularly turn into alcoholics. For the twenty per cent who drink alcohol to be high, life scripts unwelcome tragedies.

One doesn't have to consume liquor daily to qualify as an alcoholic. The alcoholic's need is to get a high. So, whenever he tipples, he has to continue to do so till he is out of his *here*.

Alcoholics and drug addicts begin as casual users. When the repeated 'high' causes biochemical changes in their brain, the pattern of usage changes into a damaging one.

A new pattern ensues: the higher one gets, the higher one wants to get.

People who are prone to dependency also have low boredom thresholds and are exceptionally sensitive. These characteristics coupled with their self-centredness makes their 'here' very discomforting.

Boredom is an emotion one experiences when every method to distract one from oneself fails. The 'here' of a bored person is very turbulent, as he suffers from low self-esteem. Bettering their self-esteem will certainly contribute to their 'here' becoming tranquil. If they are taught to channelise their sensitivity outwards, drop their self-absorption and raise their boredom thresholds, they can experience a comforting 'here'. This obviates the need to get a high.

What is a joint?

Humans are social animals and need to have connections with others in order to live happy and meaningful lives. Addicts have no genuine connections with other humans. So when they experience a connection with anything, they create a *joint* to that thing. They create fake selves when they relate to others. At times, in order not to hurt the people they love, they mask the real person within. At times, they hide their insecurities, fears, guilt or shame with robust projections.

A Joint Is a Place Where A Connection Takes Place.

Treatment methodologies have to include getting the addict *joint* to other people. Until they are able to connect to other human beings, they will keep relapsing back into their safe space, guaranteed by their drug of choice.

Addiction is merely an extrinsic negative connection. The external factor could be drugs, alcohol, money or power. Cannabis or heroin users roll a 'joint'. All those who smoke a 'joint' don't get hooked. Only those who *experience* the 'joint' or the connection with the drug do so. Forming intrinsic connections or genuine emotional bonds is the best way out of addiction.

It would be correct to conclude that the opposite of addiction is connection or getting 'joint' with another human being or positive idea/object.

Being 'joint' to emotional bonds is probably the most beneficial connect as emotional bonds cool down the limbic system. The limbic system is the storehouse of memory and emotions. A cooled limbic system restores normal functions of the brain. When our limbic system is heated or inflamed, it leads to negative colouring of our perception, resulting in cognitive distortion of our reality. Expressing one's feelings through emotional bonding is an effective method to cool it down.

An overactive limbic system continually triggers the opening of negative memories stored in its database. These negative streams of data amplify the thumps, causing distress. Sharing them with a friend releases the trapped discordant notes and negative energies. Bottling them up only increases the distortion in perceptions.

Dealing with the discordant sounds in our head independently is simply not possible. The unsettling sounds of past experiences can be drowned by the buzz generated by alcohol or drugs. But when the effect of the substance wears off, the buzzing stops, and the cacophonous notes that never really ceased are heard again. Also, when our limbic system is overheated, the thinking part of our brain stops functioning. Sharing an emotional bond gives us access to a friend's thinking part of the brain. In a way, we borrow their computer when ours is hung and needs a reboot.

The song of life (thankfully) isn't just a flat, monotonous buzz. The variations in the arrangement of the sounds that it offers, through varied experiences, creates a melody. The changing pitch and intensity of our emotions are elements required to create our theme songs.

Life is a series of crescendos and bases. When you form a connection, you intertwine two sets of notes to create a harmony. This is the music that drowns the dissonance caused by the inharmonious notes of one's past.

It is possible to be 'high' and here at the same time. Being positively 'joint' to friends, work, family, any form of art, meditation, prayer, reading or music can achieve this state of harmony—a wonderful state of being. Cheers!

∞

• CHAPTER 28 •

DESTINY vs FREE WILL

A TABLESPOON OF WATER CAN PROVOKE A FIRE TO INCINERATE a home and change the fortunes of its owners. Only a few drops have to leak onto and stagnate the positive phase of an electrical circuit. The ensuing sparks can ignite into a blaze that can cause large-scale ruination.

This type of disaster befalls tens of thousands of homes worldwide, every year. Are these homeowners destined to have their homes burnt down?

Football legend Diego Maradona's sleight of hand went undetected by referee Ali Bin Nasser, which resulted in Argentina being credited with a goal in the FIFA quarterfinals against England on 22 June 1986. The error cost England the match and the tournament.

Maradona's 'Hand of God' must've had contact with the football for less than one-tenth of a second. It seemed that Argentina's destiny blinded the Tunisian referee for that fraction of a second.

A wrong turn taken by a driver killed over sixteen million people. On 28 June 1914, Archduke Franz Ferdinand's driver Leopold took a wrong turn that resulted in his assassination. The killing instigated a series of events culminating in World War 1 exactly one month later. Over sixteen million people died during the war. The world surely didn't deserve such a destiny.

Thousands of lives and damage worth billions of dollars can be attributed to natural disasters like tornados and

i am only a tiny fragment of the cosmic order, assuredly ever unfolding exactly as it should. With my thoughts and life choices as cause, directed by universal laws into effect, i am the architect of my destiny ✶

tsunamis. Humans have absolutely no control over these events. 'We have to accept it. This is our destiny,' says Nishar Ahmed, a Maldivian tsunami survivor.

Can the accidental discovery of penicillin by Sir Alexander Fleming be attributed to destiny? If it's so, why do we give all the credit to Fleming for the discovery?

Teflon, velcro, microwave, plastic, cornflakes, saccharin and dozens of other accidental inventions are a part of our daily lives today. Was the human race simply destined to make living comfortable with these inventions?

Alfred Bernhard Nobel founded the Nobel Prizes that honour the best in the world for outstanding achievements in the field of physics, chemistry, medicine, literature and peace. Could it be that the 900 plus winners (so far) were destined to win the prestigious award, therefore it came into being in Nobel's will?

Dr Ramesh Patel, a psychologist from New York State, thinks otherwise. He believes that Alfred Nobel who amassed his fortunes inventing and selling dynamite and ballistic missiles suddenly developed an insight into the Frankenstein he had created. He was merely trying to rid himself of guilt and change his own destiny.

What is destiny? Are we just living out a predetermined course of events? A state or end that has been decided beforehand. Are we mere puppets following a pre-decided course? Certain philosophies propound that we predefine our circumstances and the amount of suffering that we will go through in our earth lives before we are born. It may be true. This theory cannot be ascertained or falsified as there is no empirical evidence to either support or refute it.

It would be ridiculous to believe that Albert DeSalvo, the Boston strangler, was sentenced to life imprisonment because it was his destiny. According to the concept of destiny, DeSalvo was just living out predetermined actions that were not in his control so that it ended with him fulfilling his destiny—serving a life sentence.

Mass murderers receive death sentences because of their actions. They do not commit ghastly acts because they are destined to be executed. Actions cause effects and not vice versa.

The universe is bound by the laws of cause and effect. The effects are pre-set, but the causes are induced by our own free will.

Is free will merely a delusion, or do we really create our own destinies by using our free will?

It is an indisputable fact that we do not decide where we are born or who our parents will be. We simply inherit the fixed blueprint of our life in the form of our DNA. It is estimated that we have over thirty-five trillion cells. Each cell contains about 22,000 DNA segments called genes. These genes determine some physical and behavioural characteristics of the offspring. But they are not the sole determinants of our health and demeanour.

The total length of all the DNA in a single cell is about eighteen feet. It's only possible to pack that length in microscopic cells because the DNA strands are spindled onto a protein called histone. The entire DNA is not exposed. It has epi-genomes (switches) on its surface that trigger specific genes to express themselves.

A person may inherit the gene responsible for diabetes but the gene will not express itself if the epi-genome (switch) to turn that particular gene on is not activated. A healthy diet and regular exercise can prevent the gene from expressing itself.

The epi-genomes are influenced by environmental factors outside the DNA. Our thoughts and emotional states can influence the expression of the gene. Of all the factors, our thought has the greatest power over the epi-genome. Love, anger, anxiety and other emotions can alter our DNA. In experiments, reported by *Scientific American* and many others, some participants were able to alter their DNA with positive attitudes.

So even though our genes are fixed, their expressions are largely dependent on our thoughts and states of mind. We have the power to change our thoughts and attitudes. We are *not* at the mercy of our genes.

What about the predetermined homes and class we are born into? We do not have a choice in this matter. The truth is that they do not matter anyway if you see the bigger picture.

In order to understand this, we have to accept some truths: We are not at the centre of the universe. Humans are not the only matter or lifeform on this planet. There are universal laws of cause and effect that govern all matter and energy throughout the universe.

Building a dam for creating a water reservoir or generating hydroelectricity has extraordinary benefits. But a radical change in the volume of water leads to shifting the tectonic plates under the earth's surface, and gives rise to earthquakes. The victims are not destined for disaster. Nature does not single out families. It just follows the laws of cause and effect.

Why did Mrs Robinson from South Florida suffer losses when Hurricane Katrina struck? The question is flawed. It may sound harsh, but the universe wasn't built for Mrs Robinson alone. It was not built just for you or me. It didn't come into being just for the sake of the human race either.

Class, caste, religion and colour are divisive concepts created by humans and are not universal laws. It is solely our perspective of distinction. 'I'm suffering because I'm born into this religion' or 'I would've been better off being born to wealthy parents' are also individual outlooks.

Pain is inevitable, but suffering is a choice. We can choose to convert pain into suffering by our free will.

'My home burned down because of an electrical short circuit' cannot be attributed to destiny. There has to be some human error in the story.

In May 1983, our organisation undertook a prevention campaign in the state of Maharashtra. Passing by Deoli village, I noticed two young children playing with some mud in the scorching sun. There was not a single tree in sight. The barren land was parched and seemed to spring out of a painting by the Australian artist Emily Kngwarreye. Wanting to ease the suffering of the two kids, I got out of the vehicle, offered them two bottles of water and a box of six Glucose biscuit packets.

One of the bottles was over within a minute. I had a long and positive chat with the children. I carried on with my journey, thinking about the lives those two poor souls had to lead.

We halted at an 'all rooms air-conditioned' hotel for the night. I had a serious altercation with my girlfriend Gracie on the phone. She wanted to call off our relationship. Restless, unhappy and sleep-deprived some six hours later, I thought about the kids in Deoli. 'They must be sleeping soundly,' I thought.

It was the seed of a realisation. The suffering that I attributed to the kids was almost certainly just my perception. The suffering I was going through was real and fully governed by my free will—I was causing it by not letting go of Gracie.

I wasn't a victim of destiny. I was merely a victim of my stubborn and selfish behaviour. Any human being with my character defects at that point in time would have met with the same fate. My breakup with Gracie was not predetermined; it was caused by my actions.

It is pre-decided that if anyone drives into a wall at 100 miles per hour, he is likely to hit the wall with a massive force.

The force will be governed by the equation: Force = Mass x Acceleration.

If he survives the impact, his body is likely to be highly damaged. But he can exercise his free will and not subject himself to the predetermined destiny of crashing at that speed into a wall.

Effects are predetermined, causes are subject to free will. We can control and regulate our causes by appropriating our free will.

This makes us architects of our own destinies.

· CHAPTER 29 ·

The Attention Fundamental

'YOU ARE A PSYCHO,' MY ELDER BROTHER DECLARED. HIS mixed emotions showed so clearly on his face: astonishment, confusion and annoyance all at once. It was January 1982; this was his third visit to my living quarters. I had just completed my residency in psychiatry at the Sir J.J. Group of Hospitals and founded my own medical practice.

On his first two visits, my brother had generously told me about a job that he had arranged for me with a reputed private hospital. All I would have to do was to go through the formality of an official interview; his friend would manage the rest. On both occasions, even though I had not registered the time or date of the interview, I'd nodded in agreement. I hated confrontations.

But on this visit, my brother skipped the formal greetings, erupting into a rant. 'Bhai, I hear that you are working eighteen hours a day. You aren't even making peanuts. At this private hospital, you will earn ten times more for just an eight-hour shift. Why are you putting me into an embarrassing situation with my friends? I keep promising them that you will join the hospital. Don't you want a good life? If you don't want to go, then just tell me honestly. I'll understand. Tell me the truth.'

'I don't want to go,' I replied. It was the honest truth, and it infuriated him. I don't know why elders always freak out after you truthfully answer any question that is followed by the words, 'I'll understand. Tell me the truth.'

'Why don't you want to go?' he thundered.

'Because that is small. Only a hospital,' I said. I demonstrated by pinching my forefinger and thumb together as if I was holding an imaginary pea.

'I'm an institution, I'm too big for any hospital,' I explained, spreading my arms as wide as I could, to demonstrate the size of my ambitions. My brother was speechless, stunned by my audacity. Then he found his voice. I was no institution, he told me; I was a psycho.

I believed I was an institution. No one could challenge that. For someone to be as qualified as I was, to be an institution on drugs—anywhere on this planet—was impossible. This imaginary challenger would have had to come from a dysfunctional home. She or he would have had a non-childhood, survived on the streets, be sensitised to the pain of hunger and loneliness, and have an addictive personality. In addition, she or he would also have to first study and then reject psychiatry. Only someone who had gone through all of these experiences would be as uniquely qualified as I planned to be at helping addicts recover.

If faith is an unshakeable belief, without proof or evidence, I had it in pathological abundance. In myself. Always. Once I decided on something, my attention was locked, like an infrared homing missile. A miss was an impossibility. Nothing could take my attention away from my intention. Even in negative situations, it was the same thing.

When I discovered that my mother was secretly married, I felt a huge sense of betrayal. I felt cheated, rejected, abandoned and ashamed. I didn't want to ever go through the hurt of being deceived again. My attention was constantly on 'not to be cheated again'.

The force of this kind of attention ensured that I kept attracting people into my life who cheated me. Subconsciously, anyone who didn't have the potential to 'cheat' me didn't interest me. On rare occasions, when I was drawn to people who might have helped me upgrade my life or my beliefs, I rejected them.

My intention, 'not to get cheated', was very persistent. It resulted in precipitating behaviours in me that were the precursors to all the cheating episodes I had experienced. In retrospect, I realise that I was constantly setting myself up to be cheated. I was both the scriptwriter and the actor.

This single-minded focus on 'not being cheated' overran my intention to be happy. It is not our intention that governs our realities. It's our attention. For example, if I want to lose weight, but my attention is on being fat, I'm eventually going to get fatter.

The contest between attention and intention is one-sided. Attention always wins.

Our brain is exposed to over three million bits of data every second. It can only process 1200 of them. Assume there are three million marbles spread out on a football field. They are laid out in sets of 2500, each containing 1200 marbles. Only one of the sets contains red-coloured marbles.

A supercomputer will register your eye movements and will be programmed to predict with 100 per cent accuracy if you see the red set. If you do see the red marbles, the supercomputer will trigger a circuit that will fire a bullet into your head.

For ten seconds prior to removing your blindfold, a voice will boom on a microphone repeatedly, 'If you see red marbles, you will die.'

If you care for your life, what are the chances of seeing the red marbles? An astonishing 100 per cent. Why? The primary purpose of the brain is to protect the body. So the brain will create a rule, 'Don't see red.' On removing the blindfold, the brain will follow the rule and in order to avoid seeing red, will see red. This explains why people who don't want to get fat get fatter. This is why I got repeatedly cheated.

What if another person is led into the same experiment? If this person sees the red marbles, he gets a handshake. The probability of spotting the red marbles will decline to a dismally low 1/2500 or 0.0004 per cent. Why? Simply because the reward is not enticing enough.

What if the reward is increased to ten million dollars, a luxury penthouse and a lifetime of security? What would be the probability of spotting the red marbles in this scenario? In this case, though it might seem to be a hundred per cent, the probability would vary from zero to a hundred. Everyone participating might have the intention of getting this super reward. However, the degree of probability of striking the hit would vary. Scoring a hit would be directly proportional to the degree of attention a person is able to give to his/her intention.

One thing is certain: all intentions don't materialise. How do you hold your attention to your intention? Any form of negativity will divert the attention away from the intention on to negative thoughts. For example, if one wants to be successful, but is gripped by hatred, anger or jealousy, one's attention will be diverted.

In 1971, Dev Anand's hit film *Hare Rama Hare Krishna* was released in India. The film featured a new actress, Zeenat Aman, as the female lead. We were preparing for the Cambridge 'O' level examinations in school then. Mazhar Khan, my schoolmate, after seeing the movie, declared to the group, 'I'm going to marry Zeenat Aman.' We were just kids in school. The exam fever has affected him badly, we all concluded.

Over the next decade, Zeenat Aman zoomed up the charts to become one of the most sought after actresses in Bollywood. And fourteen years after he'd made the announcement, Mazhar got married. To Zeenat.

Later on, they had a disastrous marriage because his intention was only to get married. If he had intended to also have a happy marriage, it could have been a different story.

Anything is possible. If you can positively visualise your intentions in detail and feel as if the event you're looking forward to has already happened, it will happen. If you can be at the end point now and then hold your attention on to your intentions, it will happen.

I was an institution in my mind even while I lived off the kindness of my hostel mates in medical college. My intention can be backtracked by examining my actions. I studied eighteen hours a day. Almost every waking minute. Either I was studying in the library or I was revising lessons with some classmate. There were times when I couldn't possibly study. Bathing, taking a dump, eating my meals, or walking from one point to another. These were times for revision.

I would visit as many alcohol parties as possible in the hostel. Besides eating the peanuts and crisps, I used the parties as an opportunity to make new barter friendships: transactional relationships. I would teach students a chapter in lieu of a free meal—the cheapest meal on our canteen menu. I was merely going through the motions of becoming an institution.

What really helped me focus on my attention was that I was predominantly in a state of gratitude. I was never in a negative state of mind. I couldn't afford to be. I was aware that I was the butt of jokes of my fellow students at their parties. I didn't mind it at all, for it guaranteed my entry. I laughed with them—at me. It wasn't even painful. I was the joker in a circus act.

The first time I saw a joker being mocked and pushed around at a circus, I was seven years old. I cried and cried. I couldn't comprehend what could be so funny about smacking a dwarf that the entire circus audience was in raptures. 'Baba, why is everybody laughing?' I had asked my father, teary-eyed. 'Because they are enjoying it, Bhai. Don't take it so seriously. You should also learn to laugh,' he had said. I guess I learnt that lesson very well.

Most of the time I was grateful to these students for permitting me to be the joker. Sometimes, I would feel sad. For them. They would be whiling away their time drinking and playing cards. 'Where are these guys going to be ten years from now? I know I'll be a top-notch institution.' That's what I was thinking at the time.

In my early student days, I had the reputation of being an angry young man, a 'Dada' revered for his tough-guy capers. But I'd had no goals in those days. Now my attention was so firmly set on my goals that I didn't even recollect my 'powerful' days. All I could see was that I was on my journey to becoming an institution.

If creation is a painting, gratitude is the canvas, attention is the paint, and compersion (the feeling of joy that one has on experiencing another's joy) and bravery are the brushes.

If a person joining a gym has compersion for those who have great bodies, he is likely to develop an admirable body of his own. If he feels jealousy towards people with good musculature, he is unlikely to develop a good physique. His jealousy is going to distract him by sending him into a negative zone. In his negative state of being, his thoughts and actions will be governed by his jealousy. Feeling good for those who have what you desire will make your desires come true.

Make any intention and hold your attention to it. It will transpire. People may ridicule you. They may say that it is impossible. If you feel fear, hold the brush for your painting bravely. Paint despite the fear. You will create your Mona Lisa.

CHAPTER 30

A Conditioned Tool for Control

SCENARIO 1: MOTHER AND CHILD: 'EAT THE VEGETABLES. STOP making that face. Do you know that thousands of children are dying of starvation in Ethiopia? And you don't want to eat your food? You should be grateful to God for what is on your plate. Don't you have any respect for food? Do you really want to be a bad boy and trouble your mother? Eat!'

SCENARIO 2: Husband and wife: 'Shut up! You have to listen to me. You know how hard I work to keep this family going. I bring in all the money. I sacrifice so much for you and the kids. You have no appreciation for my suffering. Do you think I really deserve this behaviour? Is this what your parents have taught you? They haven't taught you to respect your husband. You sit at home all day, doing nothing. You should be ashamed of yourself. I am the only husband who will tolerate a substandard wife like you.'

Variations of these monologues are being uttered in thousands of homes, worldwide. In scenarios like these, the child will almost always eat the vegetables. And the wife will let herself be cowed down.

Why? Simply because they allow themselves to be manipulated into believing that they are going to break a moral contract or do a 'bad' thing. They feel guilty. They feel culpable or responsible for an anticipated wrongdoing. When you feel guilty, you give away control to the other person.

In scenario 1, if you really cared about starving children, the right thing to do would be to pack the food and send it to Ethiopia.

In scenario 2, the right thing to do would be to invite the husband to sit at home doing the *nothings*.

Nothings like—

- Keeping the home tidy and clean
- Preparing the children for school
- Cooking all the meals
- Washing the dishes
- Doing the laundry
- Buying vegetables and other food items
- Feeding the pets
- Cleaning the bathrooms
- Watering the plants

While he would go to work, behave rudely all the time, be glued to a sports channel, sit on the sofa, and fart.

The standard definition of guilt is an emotion we experience when we feel that we have violated a moral contract.

There is a more accurate definition:

Guilt is a conditioned tool deployed to control you.

In ancient times, guilt was a necessary development to control savage populations. Followers of religious books proselytised to thousands of others. The concept of guilt fiercely flourished as it benefited certain sections of the population.

It also helped the spread of religions. Would it be correct to assume that a sizeable portion of the donations to religious institutions through the ages have been motivated by guilt and shame?

It's not advisable to feel guilty if you really want to be a better human being. Feeling guilty ensures that you repeat the action again—because it keeps your attention on your wrong-doing. You keep thinking of what you shouldn't have done. If one keeps thinking, 'I don't want to be fat', in all probability he or she will get fatter. In order to lose weight one should want to be thin and not want to be 'not fat' or feel guilty about overeating.

Susan wanted to lose weight and decided to give up chocolates. One night, when she saw a slab of chocolate in the refrigerator, she tried to resist the temptation, failed, and had a small piece. She then started feeling guilty and beat herself up for not sticking to her weight-loss plan. What happened a few minutes later? The chocolate was in her hand. She gobbled down the entire bar.

On another night, the same temptation resurfaced. She gave in to temptation again and had a small piece. This time she didn't feel guilty about eating it. She told herself that it was the wrong thing to do. She simply decided not to do it again. She didn't.

When one does something wrong, one shouldn't feel guilty. The following sequence of thoughts may follow:

'I'm feeling guilty about slapping my wife.'

'I shouldn't have done it.'

'I wouldn't have done it if she hadn't provoked me.'

'She shouldn't have provoked me.'

The guilty party may constantly have recurring cycles of thought: 'I shouldn't have slapped her' accompanied by a corresponding justifying subconscious thought, 'She shouldn't have provoked me.' At the slightest provocation in the future, he is likely to repeat a violent act again—his mind will now constantly look for signs of provocation to justify the misconduct he is guilty for.

Instead, what if he accepts the fact that he shouldn't have struck her? And understands that he has an anger management issue. Then genuinely asks her for forgiveness, being fully accountable for his action, and deciding never to repeat it again. Chances are far higher that he will not repeat the act again.

The key thing is not to repeat the behaviour again.

When someone is trying to make you feel guilty, be aware that they are trying to control you. People who give guilt trips are not bad people. The mother wanting to guilt her child into eating vegetables is not doing an immoral thing. She has learned an easy way to make him comply. Like her, all those who use guilt have learnt that it is a powerful tool to control another human being. It is a short cut. You cut it short.

∞

• CHAPTER 31 •

the FIFTH DIMENSION

'PAPA, YOU CAN SHOOT YOURSELF IN THE HEAD AND STILL be alive,' said Nita Arora excitedly.

'Go to sleep now. We will talk about this later,' her father smiled as he went into his room. He was aware of Nita's need to discover or invent something ever since she had been introduced to the sciences in school.

The senior Aroras, both doctors, were entirely preoccupied with running their nursing home at Colaba in Mumbai. The only time little Nita spent with her parents was on Sunday evenings.

On Sunday afternoons, the senior Aroras went to the racecourse. After the races, they would pick up their daughter from home and follow a three-hour drill. A visit to the Hanuman temple was followed by a ride in a horse-drawn carriage from Nariman Point to Chowpatty. The routine was rounded off with a quick vegetarian dinner at a restaurant nearby.

On rare occasions, she was permitted to accompany her parents to the racecourse. Her intention to do something outstanding came into sharp focus at the Mahalaxmi Racecourse.

Dr Ramesh and Dr Beena Arora were the co-owners of the thoroughbred Moon Rider that was participating in race no. 364 for the Bharucha Trophy. It was her first look at a real race.

The commentator's voice boomed: 'Loaded. The last competitor to step in will be Darling.'

An excited Nita adjusted the focusing wheel on her Steiner binoculars. She was growing restless.

Then the sound of a buzzer started the commentary. 'Starters orders and away they go for the Bharucha Trophy.

'Taking a flying start there is Invisible and as they settle down to race, Boxer takes the lead and on the side is Chote Nawab, followed by Gallant Creek, Dr Corto and Moon Rider. Submarine is in the sixth position followed by Darling.'

Nita's heart thumped faster. The surge of blood rushing through her veins made her hands shake, as she tightly gripped her field glasses. She shouted, 'Come on Moon Rider, go go go.'

The commentary continued, 'As they go to the 800-metre marker, Boxer is the leader followed by Chote Nawab, Invisible, Dr Corto, Darling and Gallant Creek.'

Nita's hands were wobblier now. When the view through the binoculars became unsteady, she let them fall around her neck. Her excited cries could be heard over the others in the V.I.P. box. She repeatedly punched her fists in the air.

'Come on, Moon Rider!!'

The voice on the sound system speeded up the pace of the words to match the speeds of the horses, 'As they come round the bend, Chote Nawab, with Purtu Singh on board, takes the lead from Boxer and Invisible. Gallant Creek has gone on the inside rail.'

Nita noticed Moon Rider lagging behind. She called out half-heartedly, 'Come on, Moon Rider.'

The commentary continued, the booming voice mingling with the cheers of the onlookers, 'With two furlongs left to go, it's Gallant Creek on the inside rail coming alongside Chote Nawab.'

Moon Rider was falling behind. Nita slapped her thighs in frustration, and turned her back to the course.

She could see and hear almost everyone screaming animatedly. The cheers got louder as people in the crowd turned their heads slowly, in unison, towards the winning post, tracking the horses.

Over their cheers and yells, she heard the muffled commentary, 'It's Chote Nawab who hits the front. Boxer has no more to give. Here comes Gallant Creek on the outside! Gallant Creek is trying to grab the front but it's Chote Nawab. Gallant Creek and Chote Nawab cross the line neck-and-neck.'

Soon the crowd's roar quietened and a hush settled over the race course as all the spectators waited for the results of the photo-finish.

After thirty seconds, the speakers crackled to life. The commentator announced the results to a sea of cheers.

'The winner is Chote Nawab.

In second place is Gallant Creek.

In third place is Invisible.'

Then, after a long pause, he adds matter-of-factly:

'Also ran: Darling, Boxer, Moon Rider, Dr Corto and Submarine.'

Nita's eyes widened. 'Also ran?' she said out loud.

'Also ran!! Moon Rider was just an "also ran".' His freaking name didn't even figure in the race, she thought. And she said, 'I AM NEVER GOING TO BE AN ALSO RAN. Whatever I do in life, I am not going to be an also ran.'

Later, on their customary horse-carriage ride, she asked her father, 'Papa, are we an "also ran" family?' But Dr Ramesh was in no mood for a conversation. He had bet a hefty sum on Moon Rider and lost.

'Papa, I'll never be an "also ran" daughter,' she announced, tightly squeezing his hand as she laid her head in his lap.

Her quest for excellence was soon mirrored in all her examination results and in her obsession for discovery. She began her mission by spending hours with needles and a prism, 'There has to be one law of reflection or refraction that has not been discovered yet.'

'It would be easier if I was born before Mr Snell. Snell's law is such a simple formula,' she concluded before she brought her love for prisms to an end.

But a month later, she realised that her original discovery had not yet been invalidated. That she could shoot herself and yet be alive.

'Papa, you have to listen to this discovery. Concentrate. Please, Papa. Our family name is going to be in physics text books! You have to help me with this,' she pleaded excitedly.

Her father did not want to discourage her. He asked her to explain her ridiculous theory.

She began, 'Papa, imagine that you can travel much faster than the speed of light to a distant galaxy. You're carrying a powerful telescope along with a gun that can fire bullets faster than the speed of light on the journey.'

Her voice swelling with wonder, she continued, 'Then you could see yourself from far away and shoot yourself. You could be both dead and alive at the same instant.'

Nita smiled, sketching a question mark with her right hand in the air. 'Then you could see yourself as you shot yourself. You would be the one seeing yourself die. Got it?'

Her father thought it over and asked, 'Nita, would you shoot yourself or would you shoot the image of Nita?'

'Damn!' Nita thought to herself. He was right.

Though Nita came up with several such theories that didn't pan out, it didn't deter her. It only further fortified her resolve to keep the hypotheses coming.

While her other girlfriends were fascinated by fashion, Instagram trends, or wasted their time snapchatting boys, she spent most of her time reading physics and chemistry books.

She was determined to discover something that wouldn't be disputed by her father or anyone someday. She did.

At the age of twenty-five, as a postgraduate at Delhi's prestigious JNU, she discovered the fifth dimension.

Her father was semi-retired by then. He looked forward to Nita's visits.

When she returned home during the summer vacations that year, she had to tell him all about it on the very first day. She raced through everything else that had happened, bringing her father up to date, and then she said. 'Can I explain to you what the fifth dimension is?'

'Go ahead,' he said, smiling.

'I'll begin with the first dimension. What is the first dimension? Drawing a line on a paper would give me one dimension. Correct?' she said enthusiastically.

Dr Ramesh nodded.

'If I keep this line constant and create a new variable, going either right or left from the centre of the line, it would give me the second dimension. Correct?' She went on, 'Now if I can consider the two dimensions as length and breadth, and keep them constant and find a new variable, I can get the third dimension (height).'

She took a pen between her thumb and forefinger. Spinning it around, she explained, 'Three-dimensional objects have length, breadth and height, like your ballpoint pen. We perceive all objects in our reality to be three-dimensional.'

She was so intent on her exposition that she closed her eyes to think better. Then she said, 'What if we could hold the length, breadth and height constant and find a new variable? We would get the fourth dimension. What could occupy the same space as a three-dimensional object? Think Papa, what could occupy the same space as this pen? If you get it, you understand the fourth dimension.'

He reached out and gently moved the hand with which

she held the pen and replied, 'Any object can occupy the space occupied originally by the pen—anything, at a different point in time.' As he moved Nita's hand and the pen, he shifted the cigarette that he'd been smoking to fill the same space.

'Wow! You got that. Time is the fourth dimension. We can now get the fifth dimension too if we could figure out what could occupy the same three-dimensional space at the same point in time. Isn't that right?'

'What can it be?' he asked himself. 'I am three dimensional. What could occupy the same space as I am occupying right now at this point in time?'

He thought hard, but he had to concede. 'I can't think of anything. You tell me.' His daughter had his complete attention.

'Papa, you are sitting on this sofa. Think of a variable. At this point in time, what could occupy the space being occupied by you?' she said, energised by the ideas they were discussing.

'Your deductive logic up to this point is perfect, but I don't get it. What could occupy the exact space as me at this point in time?' he said, furrowing his eyebrows and staring at Nita blankly. 'I don't know.'

'You could! You could be the same Papa, in different states of mind, at the same point in time. This sofa could be occupied by an angry Papa, a grateful Papa, a depressed Papa, a loving Papa—the variables are so many,' she laughed.

Dr Ramesh beamed at his daughter with pride, 'Yes. The fifth dimension is our STATE OF MIND.'

After a long discussion they both concluded that the fifth dimension, their state of mind, was in their control. They could maintain a positive state of mind to have a happy life. The fifth dimension could override all the other four.

'Good night, Nita. *Lokah samastah sukhino bhavantu,*'

he said, giving his daughter a warm hug as he rose to go to bed.

'What does the mantra mean?' she asked.

He translated the Sanskrit into English. *May the thoughts, words and actions of my own life contribute to happiness and freedom for all.*

And Nita had a sudden, powerful thought. If we humans are all connected in the fifth dimension, we could send out positive vibrations to each other.

The first four dimensions—length, breadth, height and time—are not malleable. They are constants. However, the fifth dimension is subject to our free will, hence changeable. We could hold ourselves in the fifth dimension of our choice. If we increase our stay in the dimension of gratitude or compassion, by default we increase the quantum of the particular holding in the universe. Since everything affects everything else, others would be able to step into the dimension of gratitude or compassion that little bit more easily.

Not only would we all live more fulfilling lives, we would also make the world a better place for all sentient beings. Do you want to begin?

• CHAPTER 32 •

The SYMBOLISM FUNDA

EYES SHUT, JOE SANTOS POSITIONED HIS MING VASE dangerously close to the edge of the precipice. He had acquired the vase over thirty years ago. He bent down to pick up the iron rod that he had created in his mind for this mission. Holding the rod in his right hand, he tightened his grip about a foot from one end. Manoeuvring it like a baseball bat, he swung hard and struck the centre of the porcelain vase. Thwack!!

The vase that had been crafted and protected with such love over the years shattered into countless fragments. Joe smiled, imagining the small shards speedily disappearing upwind. Not a single identifiable piece remained.

'I'm feeling so much better, Ras,' he said, opening his eyes slowly.

Ras was humming Marley's *'Lively up yourself'* with his eyes closed. His body was perfectly still. Seen from the back, he appeared to be an exotic promontory jutting out from the beach, as his long sand-coated dreadlocks cascaded down the length of his back, spreading out on the sands. Anyone who saw him from the front would see the faint resemblance to Bob Marley—a heftier version draped in red, black and yellow.

About an hour ago, Joe Santos had heard the '75 classic, *'No woman, no cry'*, being strummed on a guitar. He followed the sound to this Rastafarian, who sat close to the shoreline, far from the crowds. Joe had sat down nearby, waiting for the singer to reach the last line of the reggae song.

The colourful outfit bore darker shades of the hues of the sunset. Joe, after a long time, found himself inhabiting the here and now. He could feel the positive vibrations running through the melody. It was as though the song was mildly caressing his body. Bob Marley's quote, 'One good thing about music, when it hits you, you feel no pain', was so true. Joe came out of his reverie only when the singing stopped.

'Hi! I'm Joe. You are?' Joe said, extending his hand.

'It nah matter bredda, all of life is one…But if ya need one, call mi Ras. Tell mi bredda, what brings ya here, on deese beach front. Ya nah want no party? Ya left da girls far behind!' Ras smiled, and then he looked closely at Joe. 'Lively up yourself, bredda, ya look like ya stress yourself.'

'My wife left me. I'm feeling lost. I can't handle this emptiness, this vacuum,' Joe said, sketching an ellipse on the centre of his chest with his forefinger. 'Can you help me? I don't know what to do.'

'Is this da first time ya felt dis space inna ya chest, bredda?' questioned Ras, gently laying the guitar down beside him on the sand.

Joe gave it serious thought. He had felt exactly the same vacuum, that emptiness, in his chest about three years ago, when his childhood sweetheart had ended their relationship. He told Ras that story. Something about Ras made it easy to tell him things.

'Ya felt dis many times? Ya? Try fi remember, when ya felt like dis fi di first time ever, bredda,' Ras asked, gently touching Joe's shoulder.

Joe had felt this hollowness many times before. On and off. When he was in a relationship, he never felt the void. It seemed that the void simply didn't exist. Whenever a relationship ended, the feeling of emptiness would invariably return.

Straining his mind, he remembered the first time he had ever experienced a void. He was only seven years old. When his parents were saying goodbye to him at the gates of his boarding school, he had fallen to the ground, lying flat across their feet, and started to cry. The afternoon sun cast a shadow of their entanglement on the ground in the form of a twisted cross.

Clasping his mother's leg with both hands, he had pleaded, thirsting for her love, 'Please Mama, don't leave me and go. I'm feeling scared. What did I do wrong? Why are you sending me away from you? I promise I'll be a good boy. Please Papa, don't do this. I am sorry for everything. Take me home with you.'

'Don't be a baby. You're a big boy now, Joe! You'll be back home for your winter vacations in a few months. Okay!' said his father calmly. Joe started wailing so hard that his little body shook. When he began hitting himself with his hands, the school matron firmly separated him from his mother. She told his parents to leave, declaring, 'Don't worry, some kids take a little time to adjust. Young Joe will be fine soon.'

His tears clouded their departure. The only people who could protect him were leaving him behind, at the mercy of this terrifying, insensitive matron. He felt scared, rejected, helpless and abandoned. As he was being steered to his new home, a dormitory, he sensed a vacuum developing inside his chest. 'God! What wrong have I done?' he said looking skywards. It felt as though life was being drained out of his body.

That was the first time he'd felt an emptiness inside him. It was the same feeling that he was feeling now too.

'Bredda, mi make ya fine soon. Do as mi say. Mi learnt dis art at Shashamane, our Rastafari capital. Dis empty space you speak of mi bredda, you can make it go away. Tell mi, if ya have to describe dis void. Dis space, whaa ya see?' Ras asked, his dreadlocks twirling when he moved his head.

Joe stared at Ras, puzzled. Ras continued to push Joe to describe the shape occupied by the vacuum. Outlining the area of void on his chest, Joe drew a 'V' on it with his forefinger and thumb. 'It's like the void is enclosed in a container. Broad at the top and narrowing down at the base of the chest.'

Joe had never noticed before that the void he was so familiar with was encased in a receptacle that had a definite shape. It had a shape!

Ras continued probing. 'Feel hard mi bredda. Does dis have a lid? Why dis no bottle? Why dis no tin? What is dis shape? Don't think mi bredda, close your eyes and feel deese questions.' Joe closed his eyes and earnestly began searching for the answers.

He was certain that it wasn't a bottle because the base was much wider. It did not require a lid, as the space was absolutely blissful and calm. Anyone who would step into that space would feel so happy that leaving wasn't an option. They would want to stay there indefinitely.

It was like a beautiful vase. The exteriors were enticing, stunning like a Ming vase. The chamber promised a heavenly experience as it held only innocent love.

The discovery surprised him. 'Ras, it's a beautiful Ming vase that holds a loving space!'

'Mi bredda, ya feel dis space off and on. Close ya eyes. See dis Ming vase…and break it in your mind. Smash di vase into million shards. Ya can break it. Mi burn fire wid me positive vibrations by shaking mi dreadlocks. Ya break dis vase with di mind. Mi Rastafari friend called it symbolism deestruction. Try dis. Ya will be free.'

Joe did exactly as Ras suggested. He visualised the Ming vase, imagined the iron, and pictured the blow that smashed it into bits. It worked. He felt no void. It was almost like a miracle cure—instantaneous!

Ras was no miracle man. What he had learnt at Shashamane, from his friend, can be explained scientifically. Our left brain deals with thought and linear thinking, including math and science. The right brain deals with visuals, imagination and holistic awareness; it bears the insight centre.

Therefore, the more you think about a mental problem, the more likely you are to activate the left brain and the less likely you are to get insight into the problem, because the insight centre is on the right side of the brain.

Ras activated the right side of Joe's brain by getting him to give a visual to his void. This engaged him in a holistic awareness, increasing the blood supply to the right brain where the insight centre is located.

If anyone is feeling a strong negative emotion, the best thing to do is to try to give the emotion a visual first. Then the visual can be transformed into a three-dimensional physical object. What is its shape? How big is it? Does it have a colour? Are the edges rough, smooth or sharp? Does it have a smell? Is it hot or cold to touch?

You can imagine any negative emotion as a three-dimensional object, perceived by as many senses as possible. Then you can run through the following steps:

1. Change the location of this three-dimensional representation of the emotion. Imagine that it's outside the body.
2. Imagine the object a bit further away, about two feet away from the body. (This will mildly decrease its negative effect.)
3. Imagine the object at a safe distance: far away, where it is not even slightly threatening.

4. Imagine it shattering. Its tiny fragments shooting away from you into nothingness.

Repeating the exercise three times is sufficient. Even for the really intense emotions.

Our brain is just a three-and-a-half-pound mass of fat that does not have the ability to differentiate between what is real and what is imagined really well.

This method is a great stress buster. Try it to believe it. With any negative emotion. Any time.

· CHAPTER 33 ·

ANGER & PLAYING DEAD

ANTONIO RUSSO HAD THE REMARKABLE DISTINCTION OF destroying any relationship with a single interaction. He was the most notorious undergraduate student studying at The Humanitas University in Milan.

Though he had never been violent on campus, his 6'4' beefy 96 kilo structure intimidated his classmates. It was rumoured that his grandfather was an important person in the Sicilian Mafia.

His only friend was Dr Giovanni from The Humanitas Research Hospital nearby. Antonio had confided to him that in the previous semester break, he had brandished a Beretta 70 at some assassination in his hometown, Mussomeli. Fortunately, he didn't pull the trigger. He was fully aware that if he had fired the shot, his career in medicine would be over. He had vowed in church that he would never see a gun again. That he would never lose his temper again. Jesus could test him.

Just an hour prior to his second semester anatomy examinations, it seemed as if Jesus had granted him his wish.

He had entered the university cafeteria to have a cup of coffee. As he approached a table, everyone seated got up and left. Everyone, except for Joshua Paul, a student from the Philippines. Joshua had his eyes closed and was mumbling to himself, 'The corpus callosum is a thick band of nerve fibres that connects the two hemispheres of the brain. It transfers…it is a conduit…it communicates…'

Unexpectedly, he banged his fist on the table and continued in a guttural voice, 'Shit! I've forgotten everything. My mind is blank. I never wanted to be a doctor. My parents want me to be a doctor like them. I want to go back home. Shit!!!! I DON'T WANT TO BE A DOCTOR...I DON'T WAN...'

Antonio interrupted him sternly, 'Hey Signor! Relax.' Then, after a momentary pause, he said a little louder, 'You are disturbing the others, idiot!'

Joshua retorted back defiantly, adding a nasal twang, 'What will you do, Mr Cosa Nostra?' Instantly, there was a hush in the cafeteria. Antonio gave him the evil eye as he got up and came closer. Wanting to avoid confrontation, Antonio tried to placate Joshua saying, 'I will do nothing. Now sit down.' He turned his gaze downward, pretending to read his notes.

Joshua poked him lightly in the chest and teased him, 'If you are going to do nothing, then why the bravado in the first place, mafia man?'

An outraged Antonio looked around the cafeteria for someone to tell this five-foot-nothing fellow of the danger he was inviting by angering Antonio. No one met his eye, as they were too scared to look up. The silence got louder and the others could now hear themselves breathe.

Antonio visualised holding a puny Joshua against the canteen wall, his fist flattening Joshua's nasal bridge and blood splattering all around. Then quick flashes of the police coming into the campus. Court scenes. Jail. He decided to do nothing. He was still.

The students were convinced that Joshua had a death wish as they watched him taunt the angry Italian. Shaking the chair he was seated on, Joshua sang in a nasal voice, 'Mafia man, mafia man, say what you will do to me, mafia man?' The angered Italian felt like smashing his hands together with Joshua's face held in between his palms. His heart was pounding adrenaline. His jaw muscles locked as he crossed his arms across his chest. He could already see Joshua's disfigured face in his mind.

Thoughts of his medical career terminating flooded through his mind. He decided not to fight. As he got up to walk away, Joshua tugged at his shirt, 'You are such a pussy, mafia man. Do something, Mr Cosa Nostra.'

Antonio was now certain that this was a test by Jesus. He couldn't believe that even a madman would take him on. He softened his voice and apologised. 'Sorry man, I'm really sorry.'

Joshua got more charged. 'I accept your apology but if you can't do anything, why threaten me mafia man?' Then he broke into a dance, imitating a horse, twiddling his thumbs at Antonio, 'The godfather is scared of me.'

For the next minute or so, Joshua kept provoking him by singing in that irritating voice over and over, 'Mafia man…mafia man.'

Antonio's mind was twisted in rage. His thoughts alternated at rapid-fire speed between his desire to complete his medical career and his desire to teach the Filipino a lesson. 'This is a test, Antonio,' he kept repeating to himself as he left the cafeteria, exasperated and furious.

It took another five minutes for the storm in his sternum to subside. As his blood pressure and physiology returned to normal, he noticed that he was feeling proud. For the first time in his life he felt victorious in defeat. He had defeated anger.

What is anger?

Anger is a normal human emotion. It can be positive or negative. When one is controlled by anger, the consequences are disastrous. However, if one is in control of anger, it can be beneficial.

When one is controlled by anger, the activity in the

mid-brain increases. (This is the region where emotions and memories are stored.) This necessitates an increase in the blood supply to the region. As a consequence, the thinking part of the brain gets less blood supply and its efficiency drops. Sometimes it can even lead to a temporary shutdown of the thinking part of the brain (the prefrontal cortex). This part of the brain is less developed in lower animals.

When the thinking part of the brain is not available, then one behaves like a lower animal and becomes ferociously territorial. Angry people shout, scream and lash out like wild boars or saltwater crocodiles. When a person is angry, his tantrums make people move away and there is more physical space around him.

It may be difficult to comprehend the fact that while a person is angry, he is actually enjoying its power. People around him move away giving him more physical territory. He loves the extra territory, just like lower animals do. Though, inevitably, the actions will be regretted later—when the blood supply to the prefrontal cortex is regularised and thinking is restored. When he becomes a human again.

The negative emotion behind anger is fear. Angry people live in fear. They are the people who need the most help and get the least, as their thuggery pushes people away from them.

When two people are angry with each other, they will continue to stay that way till one of them gives in to fear. If a couple are angry with each other, the anger will keep escalating until one of them experiences fear. It could be the arrival of a police team or statements like, 'I want a divorce. Calling my parents now.'

A simple decision like the one Antonio Russo took can help us keep a safe distance from anger. Of course it isn't easy, but it's possible.

What is the best way to deal with someone else's anger?

Humans have evolved from life forms in the seas. A cold water bath has the power to lessen the negative vibrations of anger. Angry thoughts or emotions are, at a biochemical level, merely ionic exchanges between cells. If we harbour these negative chemical reactions within us, they have the capacity to clog our brains and get ingrained in our subconscious minds.

Depression in most cases is merely the result of suppressed anger. Sharing them with a person with whom we have an emotional bond releases these trapped negative ionic equations and sets us free from them.

To deal with an angry person one must understand their traits. An angry person has three characteristics:

1. An angry person assumes that the other person is deaf. He increases the volume of his speech.
2. An angry person is looking for a fight. The increase in his decibel is accompanied by aggressive body language that suggests that he (or she) is looking for a fight. They stare, squint, clench their fists, and invariably invade the space of the other person.
3. An angry person invariably lies. My father would often tell me, 'I've told you a hundred times not to do this.' Obviously there wasn't a data chart somewhere in our home that suggested he was keeping count.

If I had to guess the line that angry couples say most often, it would be, 'You have never loved me.' A close second would be, 'You are selfish.'

These are the characteristics that I look out for to confirm if someone is angry with me. When a person seated by my side is talking at a volume that suggests I'm far away in the corner. When a person's body language displays animal signs or when a person lies.

The best way to tackle an angry person is by playing dead, by not responding at all. The angry person is likely to get angrier, and angrier, till he or she succumbs to fear.

A non-responsive wife will definitely make the husband feel insecure and enter a state of fear. His brain may be filled by fearful questions.

'Is she planning to leave me?'

'Does she have another man in her life?'

Whenever I was non-responsive, my father's anger would be diminished. I would just look down at the first button on my shirt, faking the body language of guilt.

A good way to deal with someone who is angry with you is to drop the 'with me' in the sentences. 'He is angry with me' calls for a reaction. This may not be the case if the words 'with me' are removed from the sentence. 'He is angry' cannot generate the same reaction as 'He is angry with me.' In a calm state of mind, you can think of a suitable response.

Most people feel uncomfortable if they don't react to anger. As in Antonio's canteen situation, Joshua felt that Antonio was a coward. On my journey home from my rehabilitation centre, almost every night there are stray dogs that chase my car. They might believe that this man and his car are scared of their barking. I have never felt like stopping the car and showing the animals that I am not scared. I prefer to leave the perspective of the dogs to the dogs. I use the same rationale with angry people who behave like lower animals.

A single bout of anger can change the course of our lives. It is imperative that decisions shouldn't be made in states of anger.

The best decisions I have ever made are the decisions I have never made.

· CHAPTER 34 ·

No one is stupid

BELLA WAS GIFTED AN APARTMENT WORTH A QUARTER OF a million dollars by her fiancé. But she didn't seem very pleased.

'What's wrong?' her puzzled fiancé asked.

'It's that crack in the door to the dining room,' she said. 'It ruins the look of the place, don't you think?'

Her fiancé stared at Bella. 'A chink in the door is upsetting you. Are you stupid? Do you have no sense of gratitude? This is an expensive apartment. Even if you save $2500 every month for over ten years, you will never be able to save enough to buy such a place to live in. Why is the little crack even bothering you? Can't you see my love for you? You are the stupidest girl I know.'

When you feel that someone is stupid, it only means that you can't see that person's perspective. Even though Bella appears to be brainless to her fiancée, she is not. He simply can't understand why she cannot appreciate such an expensive gift. In his view, any sane person would value the gift of a home far superior to their present living conditions. How could Bella see only the tiny crack in the door? In his reality, only idiots behave in such a foolish manner.

But what if her fiancé was aware that Bella had decided to break off the engagement? Then, everything would make sense. The crack in the door, the frown, the ingratitude, and the argument that followed. The only reason that Bella's behaviour didn't make sense to him was because he was unaware that she had planned to break off the relationship.

It's the same scenario every time, when anyone is faced with a 'stupid' human being. Whenever you feel someone is being brainless, in reality, you are the fool. Why?

'Why doesn't he take his job seriously? Doesn't he know that he has to stand on his own feet some day? We are not going to live forever. What will happen to him when we are no more? Why doesn't he get it? Is he stupid?' Parents may think these thoughts about their lazy child. They are perplexed that their 'stupid' child doesn't seem to want to emerge from inaction.

What if they were aware of the child's perspective? Their child's simple philosophy could just be, 'They love me dearly. They cannot bear to see me suffer. I am sure they will make provisions for any kind of eventuality.'

Whenever anyone appears to be stupid to me, I become immediately aware that I lack their perspective. There could be two reasons for the way they are acting out:

1. The 'stupid' person knows something that I do not know.
2. The person is operating from a sense of short-term self-interest. Since most of my decisions are based on long-term effects, I tend to see decision-making from my perspective.

Decisions based on short-term effects cannot be understood by people who think in terms of long-term consequences. They appear dim-witted in their perspective. Probably as dim-witted as long-term thinkers appear to the short-term ones in their realities.

Tens of thousands of youngsters worldwide are working in call centres. They get handsome salaries at a very young age. In India and Bangladesh, teens have a starting salary that is much higher than their parents' earnings. Are they foolish to not invest time and effort in further studies?

If they did that, they would surely get jobs with higher pay packages in the future. But their needs dictate their decisions. Short-term benefits outweigh any consideration of the future.

People are governed by their needs. Their needs, in turn, are governed by their value systems. It could be difficult to understand someone with a totally different value system. It does not mean that they are stupid: it means they have a different operating system.

Another important fact is that the human brain only sees what it expects to see. It simply cannot see what it doesn't expect to see. So even if you are being cheated by your loved one right under your nose, it might be impossible to see what's going on. Your brain will rationalise reasons to avoid seeing the reality. It will take a crisis for you to see the black swan.

Many of my patients keep using drugs for years before they are detected by their families. Why? The parents do not expect to see their children on drugs and they miss out on the key signs.

'Tell me the truth, are you on drugs?' they will ask the child.

A 'No' from the child and their fears are assuaged. Are these parents stupid? No. They simply believe what they want to believe. Even if drugs are found in their child's bags, a simple answer will turn away any suspicion: 'These drugs are not mine. Someone must've planted them.'

On a mass scale too, it's not very different. The first reaction of most governments to any problem is denial: 'This is not a serious problem.'

It is believed that the United States' intelligence had forewarnings about the 11 September World Trade Centre disaster. They didn't take the emails seriously.

'Flying planes into the World Trade Centre? It's a stupid

plan. Where is the escape vehicle?' they must have thought. It was an improbable idea as far as the Americans were concerned, because they couldn't fathom that the 'stupid' terrorists wouldn't care for their own lives. As they proved on that fateful day.

Even the terrorists themselves were not displaying stupidity in their belief that they would, after the crash, live forever in heaven. They were brainwashed into believing that fallacy. They were conditioned to have faith in those lies. If they didn't believe the lies and were still a part of the suicide squad, that would be stupidity. But they were certain that heaven's gates would be open for them, that they would enter through a fast-track lane. They may have been deluded, but they were not stupid.

The terrorist spin doctors are possibly the most cunning people on our planet. They first create a need within their subjects: the fear of hell, the need to go to heaven, the difficulty of going to heaven. Then they fulfil this need with their lies of eternal happiness by misquoting texts. They are shrewder than politicians. Politicians can be faulted and their philosophies can be discarded if their promises are not fulfilled. These people guarantee the rewards in the afterlife. One has to die to receive the reward.

They don't take this easy route to eternal joy themselves. It beats me how they convince the people they brainwash.

'This is the way to go to heaven. You go. I'll stay.' Wow!

· CHAPTER 35 ·

The Traumatic Triangle

'WHY DO I ATTRACT PEOPLE INTO MY LIFE WHO constantly hurt me?' cried Rekha Lalwani. All the seven relationships she had had with men were pathological. They took her for granted and subjected her to physical and mental abuse.

Rekha was convinced that her stepmother had cast a spell of black magic on her to ensure that she would be unhappy. When she was only five years old, she had noticed some clumps of hair below her pillow. And some black strings that had been sewn into lemons placed under her bed from time to time.

Right from her earliest years, Rekha had been ill-treated by her stepmom. She had once tried talking to her dad about it. It had only worsened matters for her. 'There is no point in telling my father anything,' she'd thought.

She hardly met her father, as his work kept him away from home for most of the day. She was a victim of her stepmom for the entire period of his absence. She constantly yearned for her father's attention and love.

Rekha's mother had died in an automobile crash before her first birthday. She had only seen her mother in photographs. Her father's efforts to make up for his first wife's absence had failed miserably. His decision to remarry for Rekha's good was counterintuitive.

Rekha believed that if her mom was alive, things would have been positively different. Her stepmom and her children wouldn't be in their reality, nor would her father divide his attention amongst them.

She constantly lived feeling like a victim. As she grew up, in her teenage years, she began resenting her father too. He pampered her with material things. He gave her everything she asked for but he spent more time with her younger step-siblings. She felt unloved and uncared for, desperate to belong to someone or something.

As victims generally do, she chose men whom she could rescue. Average, normal guys weren't appealing to her. She found them boring and insipid. She needed someone who desperately needed her. Playing rescuer to someone made her feel good, as it subdued her own victim identity.

Her first steady boyfriend was Ayush Shinde, a slightly chubby recluse in her class who had no friends. In the early days of their friendship, she learnt that Ayush came from a divorced home and lived with his totally dysfunctional alcoholic mother.

She felt sorry for Ayush and would do anything in her power to make him happy. She was excessively nice to him and would spend all her free time in his company. She showered him with expensive gifts and lengthy love letters. Ayush was pleasant in return. Rekha was never fair to herself. All her decisions were based on being nice to Ayush. She loved the idea of being in love.

Finally, someone belonged solely to her. She didn't have to share him with anyone.

She needed to be nice to him all the time. She wanted to convert him from an introvert into a confident and secure person. She believed that he would feel better and be more self-assured if he managed to shed some pounds.

For a while, she asked Ayush to accompany her for early morning jogs at Marine Drive, a five-minute walk from his residence. She would drive from Bandra, twenty kilometres away, every morning for this mission and coax him into a healthy workout. After the jog, they would go back to his home, where she would cook him a healthy breakfast. He was permitted to have an egg white omelette with a single slice of whole-grain toast.

After breakfast, she would drive him to college and be glued to him until she dropped him back home.

Unintentionally, within a week, her requests became demands. She would get infuriated if Ayush didn't wake up before her arrival. The gentle persuasion was replaced by tantrums. 'I've driven so far to help you. I love you and I want you to look good. Do you like to be fat? Don't you appreciate what I have to go through to help you lose weight? You think I love driving from Bandra early in the morning?' Her harangues became increasingly bitter.

Though her guilt infusion technique made him comply with most of her escalating demands, Ayush gradually started resenting Rekha for imposing them upon him. He started to feel persecuted by her. Her mothering was stifling.

In order to motivate him, she would often say repulsive, even cruel, things to him. She would nudge his belly and tell him that his paunch looked appalling. She knew that losing weight was good for him and she was going to make it happen. By hook or by crook.

Her good intentions were interpreted by him as domination. Anger began to fester within him. She would get into fits of rage at the slightest dissent.

Ayush couldn't tell Rekha that she was suffocating him and he was trapped in the relationship. He was walking on eggshells whenever she was around. On some occasions, he displayed his resistance by not responding to her calls. When her calls were ignored, she would feel angry, experience severe torment, and show up at his residence.

When he first told her angrily that he was not her pet

and that she was a control freak, she blew her top. 'You have no shame or gratitude. Selfish fatso! Get out of my life!'

Later that night, she felt sorry for him, guilt-ridden at her violent reaction. 'Baby, I'm sorry. I only said those mean things because I felt hurt. You know I can't live without you. I love you. If you lose weight, you will feel good. I love you as you are. It's for your own good.'

'Please baby, please forgive me. I won't ever tell you off again,' she would promise.

Rekha would alternate between being a bullying giant and a loving midget. This rapid change in roles confused Ayush. Inadvertently, by the second month, Ayush too joined in the same chorus. Both of them would switch roles in quick succession, from being victims to persecutors and then turning into rescuers.

All her relationships followed the same pattern: a cyclic rotation between three perspectives—the victim, the rescuer, and the persecutor.

What was the issue with Rekha? How could it be that all her relationships began and ended the same way?

There was no black-magic spell controlling her life. It was her *need* that was casting the spell over and over.

Rekha's need for a companion compelled her to be nice to Ayush. She couldn't be decent in her interactions with him. She didn't care for herself. She 'sacrificed' everything for his happiness. To be decent would require Rekha to be fair to both Ayush and herself. If she hadn't gone out of her way to please Ayush, she would also not have taken him so much for granted. She would request him to do things instead of demanding them.

Without autonomy, no relationship can be a happy one. No matter how exceptional the quotient of love.

Rekha was a victim of a malfunctioning family. She turned into a rescuer for Ayush. That propelled her into turning into a persecutor, and then she got persecuted in return. Soon the tables turned and she became the victim.

After several such cycles, Ayush ended the relationship, leaving her with a significantly greater victim identity than she had possessed before their relationship began.

She began relationship number two again as a rescuer, perpetuating the cycle over and over again. Through seven relationships the triangle got further reinforced. She began as a rescuer and ended as a victim—every single time.

How does one break out of this terrible, traumatic triangle? Being a victim will either turn oneself into a rescuer or make one look for a rescuer in another relationship. In either scenario, one will end up as a victim. The only way to break out of the triangle is to see the story through the lens of the persecutor. One should assume that one is the persecutor and then re-evaluate the events and the course of the relationship.

If Rekha changed her view point and approached her relationship with the assumption that she was the bully, she would easily see Ayush's suffering. She would experience the stifling effects her demands had had on him. She would see that her nasty behaviour and her unpleasant actions, however well-intentioned, were causing agony and crushing Ayush's self-esteem. She would notice that she was systematically decimating his personality.

If Rekha could manage to see herself as the persecutor, the terrible triangle would collapse. She would not feel like a victim anymore.

Her need to begin a relationship either by playing rescuer or victim would end. That would also ensure that she would stop being attracted to needy people. Her need to be needed would be over. She would escape her turbulent whirlpool of suffering. She didn't have to be a victim any more. She didn't need to rescue another human being who was perfectly capable of managing his own life. She could choose better and healthier relationships where neither she nor her partner had to play victim, rescuer, or persecutor. She could be just Rekha, and that choice would give her the freedom and happiness she had always wanted.

· CHAPTER 36 ·

DON'T CELEBRATE THOUGHT

'I'M GOING TO SHOOT THE BASTARD TONIGHT.'
'I can't bear to see her cry.'
'The square root of 16 is 4.'
'I love my daughter, Gina.'
'Teaching is a fulfilling profession.'
'I could have stopped him that day.'
'Doughnuts.'
'I just can't see her in pain anymore.'
'I see a broken lamp.'
'I love the moonlight.'
'I'm going crazy.'

These are some of the thoughts in Mrs Annabel Robertson's mind as she trudges back to her studio apartment in Manhattan.

Our brains have to attempt to make sense of Annabel's thoughts. It may have conjured up a script in order to make some sense of the thoughts. Is Mrs Annabel Robertson a schizophrenic? Is she planning to kill Gina's tormentor? How does 'The square root of 16 is 4' fit into the sequence of thoughts? Annabel's thoughts don't make any sense. Are these two separate conversations?

Did Gina's boyfriend break the lamp on her head while she was eating doughnuts? Did he cause her pain on a full-moon night in a studio apartment in Manhattan?

Was Gina's boyfriend in Mrs Robertson's math class?'

Ever since our brain reads the first sentence, it begins

to look for connections between the sentences. Humans are relational beings. We like to build relationships between the different data we receive.

Our brain has the capacity to relate any unspecified object, event or person to any other thing. If you want to think that an elephant is superior to a horse, your brain fires neurons in a particular sequence and you get the desired answer. However, if you want to think that a horse is superior, you can achieve that too. The only variance is that different neurons would fire in a totally differing sequence.

All of our brain, like Annabel's, is constantly triggering thoughts. We cannot be aware of all of them—about 1800 or more thoughts per hour. All thoughts can be classified into the following three categories:

1. Positive thoughts
2. Negative thoughts
3. Neutral thoughts

The brain is essentially a pattern cognisant machine and a future forecasting machine. Once it recognises a matching pattern, it invokes a thought. Since the chief function of the brain is to protect our body, it mainly recognises and pays attention to our negative thoughts. The ones with the potential to be threats in the future are given more weightage. It is a default negative setting, passed down to us through our genes from our ancestors tens of thousands years ago.

Annabel is just a normal human being. Her brain is generating positive, negative and neutral thoughts. Her reality is going to be dictated by the particular thought she chooses to focus her attention on and get influenced by. Giving attention to the thought, 'I'm going to kill the bastard' will create a different set of emotions from focusing on the thought 'Doughnuts'.

If she explores the doughnut thought, she would be likely to take a detour to 'Dunkin' Donuts' nearby.

The neutral thoughts in Annabel's mind are not even registered at a conscious level. (The square root of 16 is 4 and I see a broken lamp are examples of neutral thoughts.) This is because the brain gives greater importance to thoughts it sees as threats; they commingle with other negative thoughts forming loops.

On the other hand, positive thought generation is not an automatic reaction. Deliberate action is required to create positive thoughts.

People who cultivate mindfulness have an advantage over others, as they learn to observe their thoughts. This helps them to respond to situations and not merely react to them. Practising mindfulness and purposefully inculcating a train of positive actions over time can change this negative default setting of the normal human brain. Constructing a routine, with some of the following recommendations, will definitely help bring about the desired change.

1. Any form of meditation
2. Yoga, Tai-Chi, Vipassana, or Qigong
3. Prayers or Buddhist chanting
4. Maintaining a gratitude diary
5. Loving unconditionally
6. Practising compassion
7. Parasympathetic breathing
8. Anchoring
9. Reading a good book
10. Being kind to a stranger
11. Practising novel ways of performing routine tasks
12. Focusing on just one instrument when you are listening to a music track
13. Listening to music of a different genre
14. Practising sharing your feelings

There is an important rule in neuroscience:
The nerve cells that fire together, wire together.
The more we repeat a pattern, the stronger the pattern gets. It also means that we benefit more from the same action. Any of the fourteen suggestions can be made into a habit simply by repetition.

You will definitely realise the benefits as the shift in your default setting will increase the quotient of your positive thoughts.

Positive thoughts, however, are as useless as neutral thoughts—unless we put them into action.

Humans are inclined to celebrate thought, as it is thought that gives us our superiority over other living beings on this planet. (It is also thought that causes so much of our suffering.) It is actualisation of thoughts into actions that bring about change. Once we start celebrating a thought and examining it, the script changes.

Our thoughts are like clouds, continually passing by in the sky of our mind. The ones we give importance to come to the forefront and linger.

Our brain does not react to positive thoughts and negative thoughts in the same manner. Negative thoughts stick. Positive thoughts don't. Negative thoughts are recognised as threats and the brain starts scanning for similar patterns. The thought 'I am feeling helpless' will result in all backup files in your brain that contain data where you have felt helpless before to open up. The cumulative negativity will create a stranglehold on the thinking part of your brain. The thinking part of your brain will virtually shut down and the self-perpetuating negative loops will keep rambling on.

Ricardo received his GRE test results. It was now certain that he wouldn't get admission to a good university. 'I'm a failure' was his first thought.

Soon, additional thoughts of his failures from the

I'M MESSED UP
WHAT IF I'M THE messed up one
THIS WILL NEVER GET BETTER
never never never
I FAILED
NO ONE CARES
NO ONE LOVES ME
HE HATES ME
IT WAS ALL HER FAULT
I CAN'T MAKE IT THRU
I'M SO ASHAMED
I DID THAT
I'M NOT GOOD ENOUGH
THIS WILL BE A BAD DAY
SHE ALWAYS DOES THIS
I DON'T DESERVE THIS
I'M A BAD PERSON

Dwelling on negative thoughts blows them out of proportion and become a raging bull inside my head. If i can remain mindful of this, i can drop the baggage and find certainty from my actions instead *

past flooded through his mind. Thoughts about failing to qualify for his sports team in school, the betrayal by his first girlfriend, the absence of love from his parents, etc. He was now looping in all his past failures. Twenty minutes later, he was absolutely miserable and hopeless. Celebrating a negative thought turned Ricardo's mind space into a gloom-ridden battlefield. The primary shot (thought) didn't do much damage; it's the secondary shots emerging from the past that sealed his doom.

Even celebrating positive thoughts don't always have healthy outcomes.

When Michael decided to quit smoking cigarettes, his Facebook status marked the celebration. 'I am going to quit smoking tomorrow' was his update. Michael's thoughts were consumed by the fact that he had announced it to all his friends. His brain was full of anticipation. It started firing neurotransmitters like dopamine that are associated with expecting rewards. Michael began sensing the gratification. He felt delighted by his declaration and was consumed by the effects of the neurotransmitters. The thoughts themselves created such good feelings that he didn't really need to stop smoking to feel good anymore.

The very next day he took down the post. It is needless to add that Michael is still smoking.

I, too, remember several occasions when I had positive thoughts but when I didn't put them into action, they were compensated by other positive thoughts.

For example, I had a positive thought to take my friend, Keshav Palita, on a holiday to Paris. I celebrated the thought for several minutes. It further generated positive thoughts about how we would travel to the Franklin D. Roosevelt metro station and head straight for the sumptuous steak at Le Relais de l'Entrecote. Followed by thoughts of purchasing LED lights from Castorama in La Défense for my home.

My wife would be overjoyed by their lustre and the decline in our electricity bills. I don't remember the other thoughts that followed at that time.

Eighteen months later, when I was going to Paris again, I remembered the previous thought of taking Keshav to Paris. This time I didn't waste any time celebrating the thought of Keshav and me holidaying in Paris. I phoned him immediately and told him to get his Schengen Visa organised. Two weeks later, we were eating the fixed menu of salad, french fries and medium rare strips of steak at the Le Relais de l'Entrecote.

All gyms worldwide are aware of this pattern. Their annual membership schemes offer huge discounts, but they do not add a single locker to the existing facility. They know that whoever buys into the 'annual membership' is also going to be celebrating thought—and will stop coming soon.

Do not celebrate thought. Celebrating the negative ones only cause us to suffer by forming never-ending negative loops. Celebrating the positive ones lead to inaction.

Celebrate positive action.

• CHAPTER 37 •

The Imagine-It Programme
The Power of 2 Per Cent

CAN WE CONVINCE DR BRIAN MARTIN, A SUCCESSFUL radiologist from Dallas, to spare two hours of his time, just once a month, to offer his expertise on the internet—for free?

He would have to devote two hours to diagnosing x-rays uploaded on the IMAGINEIT website. The x-rays would have been already uploaded, along with a synopsis of the patient's brief history by general practitioners from far-fetched towns and villages in developing nations. The differential diagnosis made by Dr Brian would be axiomatically forwarded by a computer app to another radiologist on the IMAGINEIT site. The second radiologist would reconfirm the diagnosis and then forward it to one of the appropriate specialists in the IMAGINEIT database, who was currently online. The specialist would use Dr Brian's radiological diagnosis to type out his recommended treatment, which would be automatically transferred through the internet to the local doctor in the developing country.

He could choose to make a free call and directly communicate with the local doctor. The calling app would automatically translate, in real time, the voice of the caller into the receiver's language, using perfect dialect. If he wrote a prescription, it would be routed to a local pharmacy in the country of origin of the x-ray. The pharmacy would transcribe the pharmaceutical or generic names of medicines into the brand names available, and send it back to the local doctor who first uploaded the x-ray. The village or town doctor would use this information received on his mobile phone, correlate it with physical signs and symptoms of the patient, and tweak the recommended treatment.

Most people living in remote corners of developing nations do not have the means or the access to medical facilities that are available in the cities. Dr Brian's two hours would change the course of diseases and the inevitable suffering they cause in over hundred homes every year. Can you imagine the benefit of these computer apps if IMAGINEIT could enroll just 2 per cent of all the currently qualified radiologists in the world in its database?

Even if only 100,000 radiologists volunteered for two hours once a month, it would mean 200,000 hours of free diagnostics. Assuming a radiologist could diagnose twenty x-rays in an hour, four million X-rays would be interpreted every year. For free! Wow.

Can you imagine the impact the IMAGINEIT programme would have on alleviating human suffering? In the year 2016, more than thirteen million children died due to inaccessible medical treatment. What if 2 per cent of all gynaecologists, cardiologists, endocrinologists, neurologists and other medical specialists volunteered for the IMAGINEIT programme? Can you imagine its stupendous influence on humanity? Even the volunteering doctors themselves would be happier and live more fulfilling lives. Just 2 per cent committing two hours a month would radically curtail human suffering.

What if 2 per cent of teachers joined in too? They could devote two hours a month answering free calls made by students seeking answers. An app by IMAGINEIT would filter and allocate the calls to the concerned teachers. The level of education and understanding of subjects could become extraordinary. Close to a 100 per cent literacy could be guaranteed in just a few years.

The troubles that spring from illiteracy, like poverty, would be abolished. Female infanticide rates and maternal mortality rates would dip drastically. Insane and inhumane rituals like female genital mutilation (FGM), widow inheritance and ritual killings would come to a halt. Household budget managements would be better and even environmental degradation could be lessened. Politicians wouldn't be able to polarise masses with their illogical and divisive rhetoric. We would slowly, but surely, evolve into a much saner civilization.

What if 2 per cent of the billion or more students too volunteered for the IMAGINEIT programme? What if each student signed up to tutor a student from a lower class for just two hours a month? What if 0.1 per cent of the world's population of seven billion people volunteer two hours in a month for IMAGINEIT's 'Be-a-Friend' programme?

Anybody who would like to share something could just click on the 'TALK TO A FRIEND' icon on the website. Four million friend hours would be available every hour to let out. The app would connect to a random friend online, maintaining the anonymity of both parties. The positive change that would occur due to this mass-scale reaching out could be mind-blowing.

Is two hours a month too much to ask for? The massive information exchange would diminish the hold of radical elements, fundamentalists and religious fanatics. Khaap systems of justice would find no sympathisers. Human equality would receive a boost. John Lennon sang over and over again, 'You may say I'm a dreamer, but I'm not the only one.' I can add to that, 'We are not the only two.'

What if Mark Zuckerberg, Bill Gates, Carlos Slim Helú, Evan Thomas Spiegel, Warren Buffet, Azim Premji, Michael Bloomberg, Elon Musk and Google were a part of the IMAGINEIT website programme? *Imagine it!*

'Imagine all the people, sharing all the world.'

—John Winston Ono Lennon

V. IMAGINE

it's easy if you try

CHAPTER 38

MY PATIENT GURUS

'SCREAM LOUDLY. SAY IT AFTER ME: LIFE IS A BITCH,' SAID Justin's father. He sat across the dining table from his seven-year-old son, swinging a single malt bottle violently by its neck. Justin was terrified of his father, especially after he'd had a few drinks. He could vividly remember every time his dad had made a scene. 'Life is a bitch,' he stuttered faintly.

'Come here,' his father said. 'Didn't I tell you to shout the sentence? Louder: Life is a bitch!' He slapped his son hard. Justin was shaking as he cried.

'Shut up. Don't display those crocodile tears like your mom does. Stand up! There! Be a man. Scream as loudly as you can. I want you to scream: Life is a bitch. Remember that.'

Justin took a few deep breaths, raised his clenched fists to cover his ears, closed his eyes and started screaming as loudly as he possibly could: 'Life is a bi...' But before he could finish the sentence, he was interrupted by a gunshot. He opened his eyes. His father had shot himself in the head.

Justin shared this childhood event with me after he'd known me for a while, during our one-on-one counselling session. A few months after that candid conversation, Justin was a changed person. So was I.

Even though I was the doctor guiding him through his trauma and helping him to accept his reality, I saw a guru in young Justin. I learnt so many life lessons from him.

Firstly, that the sum total of the traumas I'd experienced

in my childhood was not even a fraction of that one incident Justin had to go through.

My suffering was mostly self-induced, I learnt. Most of it stemmed from distorted perceptions. Thinking of Justin's experiences, I let go of any resentment that I had towards anyone. Instantly.

The strength Justin gathered from my presence was far greater than the strength that I felt I possessed to help him; his belief in me and what I could do for him was greater than my skills, or so it seemed to me.

His recovery and the recovery of hundreds of other patients have taught me how important and powerful belief can be. Their belief in me works for them.

I also learnt how powerful intentions can be. His intention to heal was so strong that he processed whatever I said, found his way to the insights that helped him heal, and built a strong life for himself.

Our beliefs and intentions create our realities. Time and again, I've learnt this lesson from hundreds of patients who have recovered from their drug addiction, alcoholism, or depression. My role is to be their friend and share the data stored in my brain.

All that I can do is to create a space of trust and love. When I share my 'fundas' with stories drawn from my own life experiences, it helps them to trust me. When they understand that I genuinely empathise with them and that I am non-judgemental about their life stories and incidents, it becomes easier for them to believe that they are loved. They heal themselves in that space.

I believe that all the people we meet have the potential to be a guru. When we are mindful and open-minded, we can witness this potential transform into a reality. Some gurus teach us 'what to do'; some teach us 'what not to do'. Both teachings are equally important if you want to lead a beautiful, fulfilling life.

Even though I have experienced both types of people and the 'what not to do gurus' like Justin's father are far greater in number, I shall restrict myself to the learnings from gurus like Justin. They have taught me 'what to do'.

In 2002, Harry, a heroin addict from London, signed up for our rehab programme. He completed the programme successfully and reintegrated back into his reality in the United Kingdom as a care worker for a community mental health unit near Nottingham. I met him a few years later and asked him what he felt his greatest achievement had been during this period of sobriety. The other patients who'd finished the programme in his batch had been proud of what they'd done. They'd told me about the houses they'd bought, the business deals they'd successfully struck, and proudly displayed their Bentleys and Mercedes Benzes.

Harry shared, 'Doc, at this place where I work, there is a patient who was involved in a road accident. His head injury caused severe mental health problems, including aggressive behaviour. No one was allowed into his room. He did not allow anyone to come physically close to him. Not even his parents. No one could dare to touch him.'

Then he smiled one of the widest smiles I've ever seen, 'I worked with him for over four months to gain his trust. And yesterday, Doc, I gave him a shave!'

He seemed happier and more excited than the others who shared their triumphs. What a mind-blowing achievement! I consider it to be the best accomplishment of the batch of '02. I learnt, once again from Harry, that non-material gains make you happier and far outweigh material benefits.

I was fortunate to meet Mr Shenoy, a parent of a patient suffering from endogenous depression, early in my rehab career, in 1983. 'Doc, you are doing great work. But if you continue to work eighteen hours a day, the way you do now, you are going to burn out. Do you think you can last, working at this intensity, for forty years more? I suggest you slow down.'

I gave his words some serious thought. I wanted to continue following my passion all through my life. In those days, I ran the rehab from my home. I was with my patients 24x7. My work began within a few minutes of waking up and ended a few minutes before I slumped into bed.

If I had not heeded Mr Shenoy's suggestion to slow down and take planned breaks, I would've burnt out within the first few years itself. As an addictive personality myself, I had to be guided into learning a more moderate way of life that would allow me to continue working in a vocation I loved for many decades. Guru Shenoy turned that key for me.

In every interaction, I believe, there is a hidden life lesson that can help us to evolve. In India, people greet each other with the word namaste. The word is spoken with the palms flattened together with fingers pointing skywards and thumbs near the chest. The greeting signifies that the greeter is bowing to the divine in the other person.

Every person we meet, without exception, has the divine within. It is only when we feel and experience this truth that we will be able to see and absorb the life lessons that flow through them.

There are other types of patient gurus too. These gurus are forever accommodating. Nothing fazes them. Their forte is acceptance. No matter what we do to them or take away from them, they do not complain. No human can match their patience, their grace, or their power of unconditional giving. Each of us has encountered them in thousands, but we just pass them by without any thought: trees!

The next time you walk in a park, notice the trees. Enjoy their beauty. Learn.

It's the student who decides not only who the teacher is, but also the teachings that he or she will imbibe. Be a universal student. Let the universe open up its classroom. Learn.

CHAPTER 39

The Solitary Universal Constant

'MY LOVE FOR YOU WILL NEVER CHANGE.'
'I don't think those negative bastards can change.'
'I can never forgive him.'
'My parents will never understand.'
'I am always going to be depressed.'
'He is exactly the same person I knew twenty years ago.'

The statements you've just read are often repeated and believed to be true. They are not.

People change. Situations change. Perceptions change. Behaviours change. Needs change. Sea levels change. Mountains change. Continents change.

Everything changes. All the time.

The only constant in our universe is change. Despite the fact that there are no constants other than change, we humans derive security from constants. But the interpretation of the word 'security' itself is subject to change—in accordance to our changing needs.

We deceive ourselves into believing and chasing illusions of stability. We keep trying to make things consistent. Since this is an impossibility, we repeatedly get disappointed and unleash suffering upon ourselves. Nothing really offers certainty. Simply because nothing can.

After a while, our illusions of constancy are shattered. We are devastated. We feel pain, and fear becomes the king.

Everything in our universe is changing. Streams and

rivers are constantly changing the ground in their paths through soil erosion, and also the composition of the oceans they pour into. The quantum of life in the oceans is also constantly changing.

What about solid objects? The table, the chair, and the floor: they seem to be permanent, at least for a few years, till wear and tear makes their changes evident.

All matter, whether solid, liquid or gas, is made up of smaller particles called atoms, which are constantly in motion—changing their positions all the time. Atoms are made up of smaller particles called protons, electrons and neutrons. These moving particles are themselves made up of quarks and leptons. They, too, are never still.

All matter is in constant motion, even though this motion is not visible to the naked eye. You can easily observe the motion in any solid using a high-grade electron microscope. Even without a microscope, we can decipher that the table, the chair and the floor are not constants. The dust on them is constantly changing. Even the act of measuring these objects will change the objects themselves—during the measurement, we will remove or add countless atoms to the object.

Our brains, too, are constantly changing. Every second, new data is being added to the brain. The data base in our brains is constantly adding inputs. Besides, the nerve cells in our brains are constantly firing.

The laws of the universe are identical for both the physical and mental universe. Additionally, in the mental universe everything is constantly changing. Our states of mind, our relationships with our parents and/or our children—these are also not constants. They simply cannot be.

If everything is changing all the time anyway, what's the point of doing anything? This seems like such an attractive option. Suppose we leave our relationships to chance, won't they become better and bloom? We might be happier human beings with healthier relationships.

On the flip side, chance could also make our relationships worse and make us more miserable. Since everything is subject to change, it's wiser to control the change by directing the change with deliberate inputs.

A plant needs daily nourishment for it to survive. Just the right soil is not sufficient. If it is not watered regularly, exposed to sunlight in the right proportion and supplemented by nutrients, the plant will die.

Similarly, just togetherness does not guarantee a good marriage or relationship. The love will collapse if not watered regularly by positive actions. The marriage or relationship will run on the momentum of love for a while. Not forever.

'The early days of our relationship were wonderful. I don't know why we are so distant now. Everything has changed now. We were madly in love. Why has this happened?'

The answer is very simple. The early days of the relationship were beautiful simply because the relationship was nurtured with daily doses of love and respect.

No matter how genuine your love is, unless it is reinforced frequently, it will cease to exist. Most people are certain that they will do anything if their partner is in an emergency situation. They will drop everything and be at the bedside of their loved one if they are hospitalised. But how many times do you think an average person might be hospitalised during his/her lifetime? Twice? Four times? Is showering attention on them only twice or four times going to be satisfactory? Anyone can make a wild guess.

All 365 days of every year, one can express love and affection through small gestures and kind words.

'She knows that I love her' isn't sufficient to keep a relationship healthy. Constant positive inputs like appreciation, understanding, respect and affection will only make our relationships evolve into brighter shades, day by day.

Any positive input makes our relationships better, helps us to grow, and generates peace within us. Whatever we love helps us evolve. Whether we love a tree or a book, a person or a brook, it's the same.

We love, we evolve.

Similarly, negative emotions like hatred and resentment cause decay and fuel chaos in our lives. Whatever the reason or the justification might be for the negativity, put it aside. It does not matter if your reason to hate is valid. When we hate, we deteriorate.

We have to keep working on increasing our positivity and decreasing our negativity all the time. Nothing is static. Life has no default happy endings.

Many fairy tales end with the line, '…and they lived happily ever after'. But 'ever after' is like a garden—it can grow only if you're willing to take responsibility for your happiness, water it and weed it, nurture the important relationships in your life and give them love, every day.

• CHAPTER 40 •

The Superior Race?

AS A BLUNT SCISSOR CUT INTO THE MUSCULAR PERITONEAL area between Priyanka's vagina and the anus, she squealed in pain. The nurses and aides pinned her limbs to the bed as a one-and-a-half-inch incision was made into her skin.

Tens of thousands of women go through this ordeal in most developing nations. The incision is made to prevent a vaginal tear. It is a regular medical procedure called episiotomy, a normal part of childbirth that helps the baby to pass through the canal easily.

Try doing the procedure on a man without anaesthesia.

The normal pain that a mother experiences during childbirth is supposedly equivalent to the pain of twenty bone fractures occurring simultaneously. The maximal pain that can be experienced by human being is when he is being burnt alive. A close second is the pain that a mother experiences while giving birth to a child.

Undoubtedly, women have a greater pain threshold and are the superior race. Women have been bearing with this pain, without any complaints, since time immemorial—for the birth of both man and woman. Then why are women constantly treated as inferiors through the ages? Why have men continually attempted to subjugate women?

If it is shocking that before the advent of Islam, female new-borns were buried alive in the Arab world, what word should we employ to describe the same thing happening on a mammoth scale in today's world? More than ten million female new-born children are deliberately killed—in India and China alone. Every year. The number is fifty times higher than those killed by the twin atomic bombings in Hiroshima and Nagasaki combined. Why is society silent on these killings?

Why do most men want women to believe that they are inferior? Forever postulating that God is a 'He'. Would it be blasphemous to use the pronoun 'She' when we refer to The Almighty?

Women are barred from entering sites of worship completely in some religions. In others, they cannot enter while they are menstruating. In fact, not only are they forbidden not to touch anything related to God, they are also prohibited from entering kitchens. There is no logic to support these rules. Menstruation isn't a contagious disease.

Is there a reason that women are being suppressed for thousands of years? In hunting societies, man's physical strength and aggression awarded him the dominating power. Is that the reason or did someone from the ancient times, when the pyramids were built, know something that scientists are learning today?

Some ancient texts have recorded information on quantum mechanics that is now being discovered by physicists. Schrodinger, Bohr and Heisenberg—fathers of quantum mechanics—were avid readers of the Vedas. According to Heisenberg, the principles behind quantum mechanics wouldn't seem absurd to those familiar with Vedic texts.

We still do not have the technology to build a modern Giza Pyramid of the same size with the same precision. The Giza pyramid embodies advanced mathematics and geometry. A pyramid based on Phi would vary by 0.025 per cent from the dimensions of the Giza. The height of the pyramid is exactly one billionth of the distance from the sun to the earth. Did the ancient Egyptians know more than what we do now?

What scientists know now is that you can fuse the ova of two women and create a baby. The same procedure cannot be repeated by using two sperms. Sperms only have energy to penetrate the ova. It is the ova that has the energy required for conception. Could it be that paranoia spread among wise men in ancient times—that man might become extinct in the future? Is it possible that some version of this paranoia fuelled this insane need to keep women out of mainstream discourse?

Is there a reason why only women are supposed to fast for men? They fast for longevity of their husband's life (*Karva Chauth* and *Vatt Purnima*) and for marital bliss (*Hartalika Teej*). Unmarried girls fast on sixteen Mondays for a good husband (*Solah Somvar Vrat*). How come men haven't been prescribed fasts to ensure longevity of their wives or for marital bliss? Can it merely be a coincidence?

Why are there so few women priests in all of the world's major religions? Pope Francis on 28 September 2015 rejected the possibility of having female priests. Even his antecedent, Pope John Paul II, had remarked, 'That cannot be done.' Why?

The myth of man's superiority has been deeply instilled in both men and women through generations. Being a man myself, I remember sniggering in science class at the slightest mention of menstruation. The girls in the class would be terribly embarrassed at every mention of the word.

Women are more tolerant than men by default. An angry man can walk out of his home in the middle of the night. A woman doing the same thing would be harassed and even be at risk of assault on the street. She has to learn to control her emotions within the confines of her home. I guess men would've been more tolerant too if they bled from their balls for five days every month. But even if men did bleed periodically, I doubt they would be barred from entering religious institutions and kitchens on the days of bleeding. As Gloria Steinem famously wrote, if men could menstruate, they'd boast about how much and for how long.

Why do men feel the need to dehumanise women by referring to them as a 'chick' or a 'bird' or a 'bitch'? 'Hey, you've got to meet my chick' is a sentence you may have heard over and over, in campuses, bars and workplaces.

Have you ever heard a girl say, 'Hey, you've got to meet my cock'? I believe that most men feel inferior to women and therefore they need to degrade them to feel superior. Women don't need to refer to men as cocks, goats or roosters. They don't need to objectify men.

Our organisation has been conducting drug-resistance training programmes in schools for over twenty-five years. We train college students to reach out to schoolchildren and teach the programme. In the first year, we had selected fifty male and fifty female volunteers. All the female volunteers completed their thirteen-day commitment. Only twenty-eight male volunteers completed theirs. We repeated the same ratio in the second year, thinking that it was a one-off thing. In the next year, all the fifty female volunteers completed the programme and only thirty-one males did.

Every year after that, we've selected one hundred female volunteers for the project. There is yet to be a single lapse. It is my personal, if subjective, experience that women are more likely to stick to their commitments than men.

Man is only superior in physical strength due to his better body musculature, and so would love sports or athletic skills to settle the question of superiority. Or racing a car in reverse gear. Their 'spatial' superiority will certainly give them an edge in the race.

In most other activities, women would win hands down.

Including longevity. Not only do female humans live longer than their male counterparts, females also outlive males in other species like chimpanzees and gorillas. How many widows have you seen? Surely many more than widowers.

If intelligence is defined as the ability of an organism to adapt, women adapt better than men. In our changing world, women have the opportunity to express their abilities. In most spheres, they are far ahead of their male counterparts. In fact, studies reveal that the intelligence quotient of women is rising faster than that of men.

Women can multitask; men cannot. Some years ago, I was helping professional musicians who'd graduated from the Land programme to record their first musical album. I decided to include a song to be played on the future occasion of my daughter's wedding. It is a very sentimental number describing her farewell (*bidaai*) from our home. An orchestra with fourteen live violins accentuated the sad lyrics, the plangent vocals.

When I played the tape to my wife, Sangita, she continued to check the laundry list. Being a man, I expected her to drop the list, gaze in the direction of the tape recorder, and listen to the song. After a while, I decided that she was disinterested in the music. But two minutes later, tears started to well up in Sangita's eyes. She carried on checking the laundry list, but asked me gently, 'Please stop the tape recorder, the song is making me feel very sad.' She was doing both things at the same time.

I don't think many men can do that. Men play in turns. 'You shut up, then I speak.'

Women have two X chromosomes. This gives them an advantage over men. If only one X chromosome is healthy, it prevents the expression of X-linked diseases like colour blindness, MASA syndrome, ocular albinism, XMEN disease, etc. Men only have one X chromosome, and are doomed if there is an X-linked disease passed on through their parents.

The female hormone, oestrogen, gives women a better immune system, whereas the male hormone, testosterone, increases the brain's threat response. This plays a major role in criminal behaviour. More than 90 per cent occupants of jails in all countries are men.

Thousands of wives worldwide have contracted HIV innocently, by having normal sex with their husbands. Their promiscuous husbands' intentions are only to protect themselves by using condoms or oral pre-exposure prophylaxis (PREP) for HIV prevention. They don't find it necessary to protect their wives. They only use condoms and have the tablets when they engage in commercial sex.

Emily Giffin has it right: 'A son is a son till he gets a wife, but a daughter is a daughter all her life.' This is not a lopsided view. What is lopsided are the inheritance laws that favour men.

CHAPTER 41

The Word Little is Not So Little

'LENGO NI MATOKEO LILILOKUSUDIWA KWAMBA TEQUIRES HATUA.'
'목표 조치를 요구하는 의도 된 결과입니다'

The two sentences above will not make any sense to a person who doesn't know how to read Swahili or Korean. Those familiar with the English language will recognise the alphabets in the first sentence—but it won't make any sense to them.

Here is a translation of the Swahili and Korean sentences mentioned above: 'A goal is an intended outcome that requires action.'

This sentence might seem like gibberish to people who do not understand English. When read out aloud, a person familiar with Hindi might know only the word 'goal' and guess that the sentence deals with either hockey or football. A non-sport loving Hindi speaker might imagine that the sentence has some connection to a round (*gol*) object.

What are words? How do we recall them? How do they influence our lives, our states of mind, and our self-esteem? A word is a single distinct element of speech or writing that conveys meaning, each 'data bit' connecting with others to make up a sentence. Words can be represented by a sound or a combination of sounds, as well as by written or printed characters set in fixed patterns.

Words are stored as a combination of phonemes (a distinct unit of sound) along with corresponding visuals. In addition, sensory inputs are adjoined, if they are associated with the word. Words like 'soft', 'gentle' or 'hard' may add tactile inputs. Words like 'rose', 'perfume' or 'rotten egg' will add olfactory inputs. The words 'sweet' and 'bitter' will add gustatory inputs. When an emotion is felt simultaneously, that will be stored along with the word.

Just for the purpose of understanding this, imagine that the human brain is like the world wide web. When we think, read, write or utter a word, it's akin to typing a word into Google's search engine and pressing 'enter'. Our brain will, in a fraction of a second, pop out the search results. Any file containing the word will open up. Just like the search engine, our brain algorithm will highlight the most commonly searched results from the past and list them in order of occurrence.

The word 'problem' on Google search results in over 239 million webpages. The same word would open thousands of files in our brain. All the memory 'files' where we have linked the word 'problem' to any other word or situation in the past will open up in our memory database. The human brain, in addition, will also affix the emotions that occurred concurrently, attaching them in the manner of labels to the memory.

The words we use to describe our feelings govern the feelings we experience.

In 1998, on our first trip to Barcelona, we got lost somewhere in a by-lane of La Ramblas. Our boys were walking with the luggage, searching for the hotel. They were growing irritated with each other. After twenty minutes they halted the frustrating search for the hotel. 'We are lost'—that was the prevailing thought. They were tired and simply did not have the energy to walk any further.

'Wow!' I said. 'This trip begins with an adventure. Let's find the damn hotel.' The mere introduction of the word 'adventure' recharged their batteries. Their smiles returned, so did their energy. Our brains have a negative response to the word 'lost', which is totally different to the positivity, exhilaration and fun associated with the word 'adventure'.

When I was a teenager, I used only two words to describe how I was feeling. At any given point in time, I was either 'cool' or 'screwed'. It is no coincidence that in those days I was either very high or very low.

The words we use to refer to ourselves are very critical to our self-esteem. All human beings err, but all of us don't respond to our errors in the same manner. The difference in responses is dictated by the words that people use to describe their mistakes to themselves.

'I'm a loser': this phrase will open up all files containing the word 'loser'. The collective emotions that hinge on the word 'loser' come to the surface all at once. The person will then react to the combined set of negative memories and obviously feel listless and defeated. However, if the person thinks, 'I will do better next time', all the files containing the word 'better' will open up. In the second scenario, it will be much easier for this person to put the failure behind him and still have a positive outlook.

There is a stupendous difference between the words 'need' and 'want'. A 'need' is something that is essential for survival. The needs of humans include air (oxygen), water, food, etc. Denying them their needs would lead to a horrible death.

'I need to meet my partner today': the phrase links all files containing the word 'need', causing them to open up from the memory database. These might include life-threatening situations like deprivation of oxygen. Asphyxiating someone will make him respond violently, with a sense of urgency.

'I need to meet my partner today' is a statement that will be treated seriously by the brain. The person will react as if his survival is at stake if he doesn't meet his partner.

However, if the same person thinks, 'I want to meet my partner today', the phrase will evoke an entirely different response. A 'want' is a wish or a desire—merely an enhancement. Thinking that a 'want' is not going to materialise might also lead to a little dejection but there won't be any sense of urgency or a life-threatening response. Having a need denied is a critical matter. Responding with violence or behaving erratically when faced with the denial of a want is just not possible.

Next time you think a sentence with the word 'need' in it, for instance 'I need to make some good friends', try replacing the word 'need' with 'want'. Think 'I want to make some good friends'. You will notice the difference in your approach, your state of mind, and the number of friends.

Is it really that simple? Yes, it is. Your brain will now see that making friends will enhance your life and will pursue the matter, but without the sense of urgency. Choosing the right word will change the experience as well as the response. Substitute the word 'problem' with the word 'challenge' the next time you are faced with a difficulty and experience the difference for yourself.

Words are very important. Most students I know have blanked out on more than one occasion while they are studying. If a student misunderstands one word that he is reading, he goes blank on the paragraph. A few misunderstood words, and she or he is blank on the entire chapter.

As the brain cannot figure out the meaning of the 'misunderstood' word, it goes on overdrive trying to fit it into context. It short-circuits its network, and draws a blank. Just like a person who doesn't understand Swahili or

Korean would go blank trying to read the first two sentences in this chapter. Technically, any student studying without the aid of a dictionary is not studying at all. There is no way that she or he will be able to comprehend every single concept that is in their text books.

We can send emails to ourselves on the world wide web. Similarly, we can also send self-emails to our brain's inboxes. Every thought that we have ever thought is registered by our brains. Every word directed to us is also recorded in the same way. All the negative (or positive) words we think, speak, read or hear are constantly being recorded by the brain.

Presume that our negative recordings are marked in red and the positive ones are catalogued in yellow. When we open the inbox, we see a lot of one particular colour. If we see more of the yellow labels, we are happy and if we see more red labels, we're sad. We can increase the positive ones simply by stopping the negative self-talk or by increasing the positive self-talk.

Making a habit of positive self-affirmations will increase the number of emails marked yellow—and therefore, you will feel happy. Your brain does not demarcate what you say to yourself and what others say to you.

Repeat any positive sentence to yourself and you can be sure that your brain will accept it. A few suggestions are given below, but you're welcome to tailor an affirmation to your own preferences.

'I am a good human being and am fully in control of myself.'

'I am a loving and loveable human and am in a state of immense gratitude.'

'I love myself and everyone around me. Life is beautiful.'

'I live in abundance and God loves me.'

Repeating a positive sentence every day (at least ten times) will make you feel more positive. Making it a part of your daily ritual will ensure its continuance. Do it as a part of your routine, either before or after a bath or a meal.

Language gives us superiority over other living beings on our planet. Language also creates colossal miseries for us, much more misery than most non-human animals create for themselves. Other animals cannot destroy the planet. We can. In minutes.

Use the less offending word when you are in a negative situation, and it will lessen the impact you will experience. If the sentence, 'I am completely depressed today' is replaced by the sentence 'I am a little depressed today', it will make an enormous difference to your well-being. The word *little* is not so little.

• CHAPTER 42 •

THE POWER of I

'THIS IS *I* BRAIN'
 'It's in *I* mind.'
 'This is *I* body.'
 'This is *I* hook.'

Even a child in primary school knows that the above sentences are incorrect. If the pronoun *I* is substituted with the word *my*, all the sentences will make sense. *I* is used to refer to the self. *My* refers to being associated with or belonging to the self.

We say, 'This is my brain', because the brain belongs to the I or the self. The brain is the physical organ and the mind is just an animated brain. I is not a product of either the brain or the mind. The brain and body belong to the I, and not the other way around. It would be as ridiculous as saying that your I belongs to a hook.

Your I can do anything. In fact, your I uses your brain to perceive whatever it wants to perceive. If your I wants to perceive Mr A as a bad human being, it fires certain nerve connections, in a particular sequence, to do so. However, if your I wants to perceive Mr A as a good human being, it uses other nerve connections in a totally different sequence. Your I is guided by its need.

Haven't you encountered people who have changed their opinions about you when their needs changed? For no apparent reason that you can credit to yourself, they have changed their behaviour. Has this never happened in your reality? If it hasn't, the chances of you seeing a striped mermaid with red polka dots are high.

'I am like this only, I can't change' is a sentence that I hear often during counselling sessions. That is rubbish. A man professing to his wife, 'I can't control my anger' is implying that he does not want to control his anger. When the same man is confronted by a set of strong policemen, it's so easy for him to control his uncontrollable anger. He does it effortlessly.

I, Dr Yusuf Merchant, do not speak Spanish. This does not imply that I can't speak Spanish. I can. If I really want to speak the language, it is possible. I can take my body and my brain to a Spanish class, attend the classes diligently, pay attention to the teacher, and do the set homework. When I have revised the lessons sufficiently, I will be able to speak the language. *Es sencillo!* It's simple.

The brain is not a static organ; its neuro-plasticity is well documented. It is constantly changing. The inputs we feed into our brains direct this change. Established neural pathways can be expunged and newer ones can be created. Anyone saying, 'I am depressed now, I think I will be depressed forever' isn't aware of the truth. Just because a kitchen drain is clogged, it doesn't mean that it can't be unclogged. There is no need to resign oneself to a stinking kitchen forever.

There are two simple rules in neuroscience that govern the plasticity (changeability) of our brains:

Rule 1: The nerve cells that fire together, wire together.
Rule 2: The nerve cells that do not fire together, do not wire together.

Why are there two rules? Actually only one rule would have been sufficient. The rule could have been: Only the nerve cells that fire together, wire together. But there are two rules. There is a deeper meaning to rule number 2. It means that the nerve cells that do not fire together, do not wire together any more. Which implies that we can change anything about ourselves, including learnt behaviours.

When we persist in indulging in negative self-talk, certain nerve connections within our brain are formed. We feel lousy and depressed. We can force ourselves to do positive self-affirmations and stop doing the negative self-talk. If we do, the connections of our negative self-talk will be severed and newer connections of positivity will be created. Their enhancement is directly proportional to the number of repetitions. If your I wants, it can change your outlook about life itself.

When one repeatedly takes anti-anxiety pills to feel calm, the brain forms a connection between the pills and a state of calm. The more the repetitions, the thicker the nerve connections between the two. Which implies quicker and greater should be the effect of the pill. However, this is not experienced by the pill popper. Why?

With the repetitions of the doses, the body also learns to destroy the drug faster. As time goes by, the user needs to take increased doses of the medication to achieve the same effect. The user will soon believe, 'I need to take the pills to get rid of my anxiety. I am like this only. Nothing else will work.' This is true. 100 per cent. Except when it isn't true.

One powerful alternative way is when the user decides to stop taking the pills and starts doing something else, repeatedly. Anti-anxiety pills work by regulating serotonin levels in the brain. Serotonin levels affect our moods, sleep patterns and behaviours. One can increase serotonin levels in the brain without taking any pharmaceutical preparations. Listed below are simple ways of increasing the level of

Ruthless and brutish as a master, my mind is a powerful ally once firmly saddled. Instead of being controlled by it, i now take charge, making the choice to steer it in any direction i choose

these mood elevators. If you implement these suggestions repeatedly, nerve pathways will be created in your brain to make you feel calm. Your *I* can and will change your brain, thereby changing your mind, your perceptions, and your behaviours.

- Exercise for at least forty-five minutes daily
- Get exposure to sunlight (with sunscreen SPF 20+) for at least thirty minutes daily
- Add milk, cheese, egg, yogurt, pumpkin and sunflower seeds, garlic, spinach, turmeric, salmon, dark chocolate, tofu, bananas, pineapples, plums, sour cherries, nuts and green tea to your diet
- Pamper yourself with a massage once a week

If you are likely to forget these suggestions, incorporate them into your daily ritual. The benefit of a ritual is that you don't need any will power to continue doing it. (You don't have to remind yourself to brush your teeth daily, you simply do it.)

If you plan to implement the suggestions for a year, you are not even likely to begin. You will stop at the planning phase itself. Make a decision to do it for just one week. If you can manage to do that, decide to do it for just a month. By the end of the month, your brain will be hardwired to a new pathway to increase its mood elevators. It will then be easier for you to continue it as a lifestyle.

I suggest the following routine. It covers the entire spectrum of serotonin enhancers.

For breakfast: Blend a glass of milk, a teaspoon of sunflower or pumpkin seeds, and a pinch of turmeric in a mixer. Drink the concoction. Next, use sunscreen (SPF 20+) and go for a jog in the morning sun for forty-five minutes.

Have salmon, eggs, chicken or tofu, or spinach cooked

with garlic, cheese or cherry tomatoes for lunch. Drink lots of water and green tea. Have fruits like pineapples, plums, sour cherries or bananas for dinner. End the day nutty, with walnuts or almonds and/or a little dark chocolate. Avoid caffeinated drinks completely.

If you and your partner can give each other a massage once a week, you will have covered the entire spectrum mentioned earlier to increase your serotonin levels. It may also spice up your sex life. If you don't have a partner, locate a non-sleazy massage parlour. (AIDS is on the rise.)

When you finish reading this book, you are likely to fully appreciate the incredible power of your I. Your I can do anything, within the permissible laws of the universe. Your I can learn to deal with any situation. Your I can change any habit. It's simply like learning a foreign language. The next time you feel, 'I can't do this', know that your current nerve pathways are making it seem that you cannot. You have the power to change your current nerve pathways simply by repeating your intended actions, over and over.

Your brain is neuro-plastic. It's fantastic!

ACKNOWLEDGEMENTS

I THANK EACH AND EVERY HUMAN BEING WHO HAS participated in and enriched my life, thereby providing me with a wealth of experiences which have culminated in this book.

I am grateful to:

Nilanjana Roy, for being an inspiration, mentor and guide throughout the writing process.

Kriti Monga, for brilliantly portraying the essence of my thoughts through her imaginative artworks.

Nabila Ankolvi and Arjun Nath, for the initial edits.

Debasri Rakshit, for the final edit.